C000090353

Saddled with Retirement

USA Quest

Paul Bunce

Saddled with Retirement
USA Quest

Copyright ©Paul Bunce, 2018. All
rights reserved.

ISBN: 9781983270895

Cover design by Paul Bunce

Copy and editorial assistance
provided by Chris Bunce

April-May 2018

Some names in this book may have
been changed to protect them from
additional embarrassment or simply
because I may have forgotten their
names. Please avoid copying
without prior permission.

More material about Paul and his
trips can be found on his website:
www.saltash.com

Dedicated to both my family and my students, without either my journey in life would have been duller, pretty fruitless and probably wasted.

TABLE OF CONTENTS

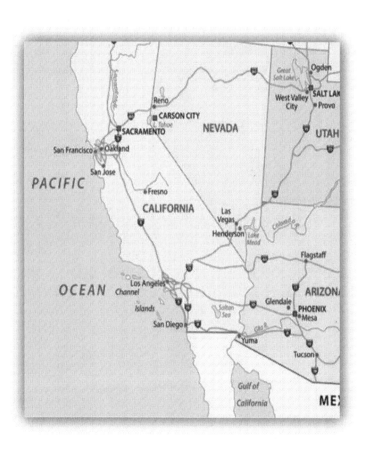

Chapter 1

Why?

The idea to undertake such a hair brained journey was the result of a combination of events that culminated in both the opportunity and the need of such a quest. The previous year a lifelong struggle with Bipolar disorder resulted in my teaching career of 17 years finishing early. This end of my teaching as a lecturer in a further education college was difficult to accept, it was not a conscious decision on my part and more a default position, given the length of the illness from the latest depressive episode.

My teachers' pension was to kick in early; in this case I was 52 years old, albeit with a much, much lower pay-out. So, medical retirement was where I found myself, however I must be honest I was totally unaware of what was going on for that year as my illness was an ugly ever present influential dark force -only kept in some sort of control by a cocktail of strong medication. The normal day to day household running and major work was heroically undertaken by my wife of 33 years, Chris, the ever-patient saint.

Cycling has always been a part of my life, either as a commuter or used to relax; it allows me to switch off in a way that cannot be replicated in any other activity. I am not sure how this works but whilst cycling I enter a zone that is akin to meditation, only different as I have a full awareness of my surroundings for both observation and safety. The additional benefit is that the link between exercise and depression is well documented as a positive influence, this I can attest to.

I had always wanted to do a long-distance cycle tour when I had retired and Europe was one of the main contenders for this, however with the realisation that I would be younger and supposedly fitter I could consider virtually anywhere in the world. The only limiting factor would be my perceived and real constraints based on time and funds available. So, after my work situation was resolved and after what felt like an eternity being drugged all the time with medication, I started to feel more human and a small travelling thought started to grow momentum in my mind. It also felt that a more significant journey on the bike may be therapeutic in my personal road to recovery.

The die was set and a link between a cycle tour and my health was established. This for someone that has no belief in the system of psychotic drugs was too good to be true and became a self-fulfilling prophecy. Then in the December before the trip it was decided under medical advice that all my drugs would be tapered off over a few months.

The jigsaw pieces were all fitting into place around me, some force was providing a helping hand to enable the trip to perhaps become a reality. Not being one to ignore an unravelling situation I could start planning, this meant sitting in front of *Google Earth* and *Garmin Basecamp* on the PC and zooming in and out on places on the world, paying attention to terrain, heat and the all-important facilities of food, water and shelter. As a basis for my planning I had decided that 5 weeks away from home would be the longest duration to consider currently as although retired I still had to help run the household with two grown up children that had moved out and one teenage daughter due to take GCSE's around May-June. With an average daily mileage of between 40-70 miles over 4 weeks cycling was also considered as a good starting point as this would allow for time for slippage and doing the touristy stuff as and when required.

Thus, between 1 to 1½ thousand miles would be the total mileage using the above parameters, so it was back to *Google Earth* with this is mind. The available methods for stopping overnight are hotel, motels, camping or staying with hosts using the *www.warmshowers.org* cycling organisation.

All these would be considered apart from camping as although I am quite experienced in cycle camping, I wanted to keep the overall weight down as I would be flying to and from both the start and final destination. Cycle camping always requires a tremendous amount of additional weight being carried, such as the tent, sleeping bag, camp mat and cooking equipment, which based on my last John O`Groats to Land End tour would add an additional 14kg minimum to the gross weight.

The use of flying to my starting point also created the problems of how to prepare the bike to meet the airlines own specific requirements that range from it being allowed to be carried in a large polythene bag to having to be in an expensive top of the range flying bike box, which incidentally could cost more than my bike is worth! With these factors considered being duration, distance to cover, method of overnight stops, budget available, airline bicycle rules it finally left the bike choice and the difficult one of location. The planet is big! Plus my small journey distance on it was small in comparison, this realisation that "continent crossing" was not going to happen, I had to think smaller but smarter. My knowledge of foreign languages is limited to French and even then, during some of my French cycling tours it is painfully constrained. I also feel that I unable to learn a language prior to the planned departure date given the limited time; an English-speaking country would have to be top of my list. However, I did not want to spend around four days getting to and from the country, so Australia and New Zealand could not be in the running-this was a shame as my experiences with being with antipodean people when I worked in London was of them being open and honest and very down to earth.

North America was now meeting a lot of the restrictive criteria; it speaks English but I was unsure if cycling in either USA or Canada was recommended or advised.

The weather on closer inspection in April/May in Canada was still too cold, this left the USA. Fortunately, I have some British friends that live in the USA, being Chicago and San Francisco. After checking weather at these locations for April it was obvious that only San Francisco was suitable and not covered in snow.

I now had at least a starting or ending point that would help me plan the now identified Southwest USA quest. Neil is a fellow Cornishman that used to work in the City of London back in the 80's with a stockbroker, and we met often to put the world to rights over a few beers as one does. These sessions were usually over lunchtime but sometimes overran into longer and longer evening events, however in my defence this was during my "BC time-period", i.e. Before Children! So, I had fewer responsibilities. Then a few years later it was time to bid farewell to Neil as he left the UK to start a new life with his new found American wife, eventually moving to the state of California to Walnut Creek which is about 20 miles outside San Francisco. Neil and I had maintained contact via the social media site "book of faces" so that my request to stay a few days was met with a positive answer and he could also take me to the airport in his large American SUV with my bike.

Looking at the map of the Southwest USA it is hard not to be amazed by the sheer size of the land which could easily be matched by 3-4 United Kingdoms placed within it. Given my constraints I could not cover all of it; I had to be inventive on what route to create covering all the areas that I would like to visit.

Then after researching that the American rail company *Amtrak* was now accepting fully built bikes on some services, it seemed that I could incorporate a rail segment into the journey, without the pain and hassle of having to prepare the bike for transit.

What in the Southwest USA do I want to see? A quick list pointed to the states of Nevada, Arizona and California that contained the attractions that I would like to visit on my bike tour.

It became obvious in my early research that the weather in the planned area would range from possible snow above 6,000 feet to baking 40 degrees Celsius in the desert areas, together with possible strong winds that could be headwinds for days on end. With that thought I decided to use my *Dawes Galaxy Tour* touring bike in place of my *Cube Delhi Pro* hybrid. The reasoning behind this was that the drop handlebars on the *Dawes* would allow me to reduce the effect of any possible head winds, and as a light bike equipped with very low "granny" gears it should make the extremely long hills more manageable. My other bike being the *Cube Delhi Pro* hybrid, although equipped with front suspension and hydraulic disc brakes does have straight bars which means that any headwind would be exhausting and unacceptable.

The easiest decision of them all on the equipment to use is the *Brooks B17 Special* saddle which has never let me down in the last 10 years; in fact, I ditched padded cycling shorts around 6 years ago and just use normal shorts for cycling with no problems at all. Although pricey at around £130, these saddles will last a lifetime and will mould to your shape after a few thousand miles. Just remember to lift off every so often to let all your bits have a good blood flow; this will avoid any nastiness you hear about on other saddles.

At the same time as planning the route it became obvious that the *Dawes* would need some newish parts to ensure its reliability on the journey, this starts with the rear cassette and front chain rings as they were worn down and both wheels as the rim wear indicators were now showing. To keep the budget down I sourced all these as good second hand parts from *EBay* at around 60% cheaper than new. The only new parts that I purchased were new *Schwalbe Marathon Plus* tyres and a chain and finally a set of double sided pedals, one side for MTB clip-ons and one side flat for normal shoes. This is because I had a hunch that some of my right foot problems may be caused by the MTB clips, this would be an opportunity to test my theory! Before long the bike was ready, although I had not ridden it in a few months so this became my full time hack bike so that it could 1. Be tested for reliability and 2. Allow my body to get used to drops again.

The route lines on the *Garmin Basecamp* software were growing and dotted throughout the three chosen states, all placed with the details on mileage and altitude climb for that segment. It was getting hard to create a route whilst considering all the attractions that I would like to see without exceeding the restrictions that I had imposed, as a compromise I may have to include some long day cycles and exceed the climb limits for that day's segment, or "leg" as I was now calling them.

I then saw some very reasonable flight tickets with *Virgin Atlantic* and after checking that they charge £65 for a bike each way I decided to buy the Premium Economy tickets as this allowed 2x 23kg packages to accompany the flight free of charge, so I would have more comfort for virtually no additional cost, a bit of a luxury I know but my phobia of flying is real and anything to occupy my mind either eating, drinking or film watching was an absolute necessity.

The journey now became tangible as it had cost money for parts and flights, my friends and family were told of my trip in better detail, I received a variety of responses, all the time knowing that I could not back out now, I had to prepare both my mind and body of what was to come. Failure to start would be a great and costly embarrassment! My own journey for better mental health was now inexplicably linked to this quest, one had to prompt the other, and conversely one could bring the other down. This was becoming a major life test for me for which I wanted to enjoy and benefit from in the years to come.

Chapter 2

The route

The route did not make sense; it was too long both in distance and duration. Something had to change for yet another re-write; I had already spent many days trying to decide on the various legs required. I had already booked the flights so that was not a variable. I was due to fly from Gatwick on Sunday 15th April to land in Las Vegas the same day at 1pm and return from San Francisco to London Heathrow on Sunday 20th May which arrives the day after on Monday, due to the 7-hour time difference being cancelled out.

I then looked at the *Amtrak* routes that were available and I could see that there was an overnight train every night that wound its way from Chicago to Los Angeles. Perhaps a bike ride from LA to San Francisco was possible within the timeframe? But checking details of previous adventurers that had undertaken this trip all stated that the wind was always from the west and that often landslides on Highway 1 being the coast road closed it and made for very long detours.

This direction was not suitable for a cyclist with a short timeslot and heading north into a strong wind. These dead ends continued with a plan that I had to head south and use part of the American Cycling Southern Tier Route across the United States via Blythe to cut across to San Diego but as the temperature at the time of the year was excessive coupled with the fact that some legs would require journeys across the desert without water stops exceeding 80 miles, this was unacceptable for a desert novice such as me. I had to reduce the risk of cycling in potentially dangerous locations.

I then approached the route planning from the train stations angle to see if that allowed something to fall into place and luckily it did. The station at Flagstaff in Arizona allowed bikes to be pushed onto the train with a departure time in the late evening arriving in Los Angeles Union station the following morning.

It now made sense to split the journey into two separate stages. One stage would be starting in my landing location of Las Vegas, Nevada and making my way to Flagstaff, Arizona. The second stage would be from LA to San Francisco via an inland route to avoid the often-disrupted Highway 1, using the hills on the west to help block the worst of the wind. Once the stages were created it became easier to plan after setting the original restrictions into the map.

So, after a few weeks researching, planning, reading first-hand accounts and watching the multitude of YouTube videos posted by cyclists from around the world in this part of the USA it started to become more than a draft.

The details of the stages were then decided as:

Week 1-Las Vegas for 4 nights to allow acclimatisation to the heat that is not present in the UK! Also, to experience both the gambling and the architecture of the strip casinos.

By the way I am not an active gambler as I spent too many years working in a stockbroker business in London and have seen that the greed of winning is often stronger than the acceptance of losing.

I would be very cautious in my obligatory limited gambling. Then Las Vegas to Boulder City to see the Hoover Dam and Lake Mead complex. Finally, Boulder City to Searchlight and then Searchlight to the small gambling resort city of Laughlin in the hot, low arid desert.

Week 2-Laughlin via various towns of which some are on the historic route 66 to make my way to the Grand Canyon South Rim continuing to Flagstaff.

Week 3-Flagstaff to LA on the *Amtrak* overnight rail service and visit locations within this mega-tropolis such as Hollywood and Beverly Hills.

Week 4-Leave LA north westerly then cut easterly inland up to the Mojave Desert which will make the subsequent north westerly direction to Bakersfield more of a downhill into the expected strong headwind.

Week 5-Travel through the agricultural valley making my way to San Francisco and finally stopping with my mate Neil in Walnut Creek for the final 3 nights prior to flying back to London Heathrow.

This was the route; it was time to fill out the details and consider accommodation and research any possible problems that could be experienced.

It was now that the butterflies started to flutter in my stomach; however, the negative ones fluttered harder than the excited one. I felt sick as the magnitude of the undertaking was now being fully realised. I estimated that I would be cycling across deserts at 30-40 degrees, hills going up to 7,500 feet (Ben Nevis is only 4,400 feet and is the UK's highest mountain) with large stretches of the journey either very remote or very busy requiring going onto the USA Interstate in some places-akin to cycling on the M25 for a whole day! The total mileage appeared to be around 1,200 and the number of days cycling was 28 out of a total visit of 35 days.

This information proved that this was within my abilities based on my previous UK cycling history but it still has so many unknowns that could not be understood until there. The more I looked at it the more nervous I felt. But it now felt so mandatory to achieve, harking back to a traditional Navy saying: preparation and planning prevents piss poor performance- the 6 P's! I need to plan and prepare like never before, my life could literally depend on it.

With the advent of the Internet and GPS systems the job of research and route planning has been made a lot easier than looking at lots of paper maps, additionally paper maps become out of date, whereas this is not an issue with online map systems. My *Garmin Touring Edge* bike GPS system is now about 5 years old but has proved itself on both a John O'Groats to Land's End ride and on a Midlands trip to Derby.

It allows routes to be created at home that follows cycle paths where available or quieter roads, these can then be checked on *Google Earth* to make sure that the route is suitable. However, it is important to check as sometimes a grass trail is suggested which can be annoying whilst on the road. As mentioned before more preparation and planning does help the overall suitability of any route used. The software package is the *Garmin Basecamp* which allows route creation and is set by default to utilise the most preferential cycle route based on the settings provided.

It will not suggest interstates or freeways for obvious reasons but as will be seen later that was not always the case. The *Garmin* GPS also provides turn by turn advance warning which I testify is beneficial when in built up areas as it gives notice of upcoming turns by beeping at you and also helps you to position into the correct lane-bearing in mind the most difficult is the left turn in the USA.

The *Garmin* GPS system covers a lot of data fields that are user adjustable, such as the time cycling, speed, distance so far, local time, height above sea level, miles to destination and finally expected time of arrival to end of days' route. Physical maps however, although they may contain old information are also required as batteries can go flat! So, I made sure that maps of the route were also included should I have to go back to prehistoric times. Now the routes have been created, tested, reviewed and loaded up to the GPS in preparation of the journey.

With the route created my next task was to investigate the accommodation to use at each stopover point. I looked at *www.warmshowers.org* and sent out lots of emails to hosts expressing an interest of stopping at their place on a specific date for one night.

Unfortunately, the number of responses that I received up to 3 months later were poor, more specifically none! This was a major worry, without the knowledge of a place to stop each night it meant that the ride was in jeopardy. Fortunately, I turned to *Booking.com* and I looked through the dates and locations that I was due to be in and looked for the cheapest motel/hotel that was available and close to my days finish point.

Some motels looked well iffy with very poor reviews-but better than nothing, so I selected cheap ones that I could cancel without incurred costs and these were booked. At least if my hosts did not come through later there was a bed and a shower at the end of a day's ride-these are important things for a cycle tourer.

I was pleased that I had achieved the main aspects of a major tour, being the equipment prepared and made ready, the route created and fully tested; places to stay found and booked.

Chapter 3

Ready or not!

It was now time to make sure that the body and mind were as best prepared as possible, it was now November and the ride was now only 6 months away and as the choice was the *Dawes* bike which I had not ridden much over the last few years I had to start some serious training on it. Cornish weather is not always conducive for cycling apart from about 2 weeks in August! I had some wet weather to get used to, on a bike with antique rim brake-blocks system which as most cyclists know actually do very little braking when used in the wet. To try and replicate the load I measured out bottles of water totalling 18kg, these were then balanced in the *Ortlieb* panniers on the rear.

Gosh the bike weighed heavy, although the *Dawes* was designed as a heavy tourer it was still a surprise once again how it wallowed around corners and took an age to pull up. The daily training route when dry was a 15-mile circuit over to Plymouth and up to Roborough returning after a total climb of 1,500 feet. When wet, I used my turbo static trainer in the garden shed and tried to replicate the ride on the *Cube* bike although without the hill element but with a major boring element in its place.

The USA has expensive health care so I looked around for holiday insurance that would cover me for cycling around and accept me for my pre-existing bipolar condition. This as it turned out was one of my major tasks. Insurance companies treated me as a poor investment, especially when I asked for additional cycling cover whilst in the USA for 5 weeks, the phone would go quiet and keyboard noises clatter at the other end followed by some astronomical quote, at this rate it would be cheaper to employ my own personal doctor to accompany me.

To not have medical insurance in the USA would be stupid- I had to have insurance. Then after days of looking I was reading an article where someone else with Bipolar had problems looking for holiday insurance and the response suggested a few companies of which one I had not previously tried. After applying with full disclosure of pre-existing and adding cycling as a dangerous activity (!) I had a slightly more favourable quote in reply.

This I snapped up before they changed their mind. It's such a shame that holiday insurance companies are so strict and raise their premiums on lifelong conditions irrespective of a no previous claims history. Now as I type this back in the UK I do feel that I was mugged and had to pay much more due to skewed insurance statistics.

The training continued although the hills in Devon and Cornwall were made much worse by the additional weight being carried, the leg muscles hurt with the regimental daily mileage. I tried longer and longer rides when the weather was better, even up to the 1,000ft. Kit Hill which was an 8-mile uphill climb. After around 3 months of daily training I did feel slightly more optimistic that I could deal with most of the planned journey although the gruelling conditions were going to have to be experienced first-hand when I got there. It is difficult to know how much training is required for a ride when all you know is the distances, too much training will leave you shattered before it starts and too little will change a once in a lifetime ride into a long drawn out nightmare.

A balanced approach was needed and I still believe that fitness is also 50% in the mind, if you think you can do it then you have a fairly good chance of achieving it. I have read that many long-distance cyclists debunk the training and prefer to let the body adjust whilst on the ride. I tried to avoid the body shock of constant cycling with my training but was fully aware that with a determined attitude most distances less than 70 miles could be achieved daily if attacked mile by mile only.

The daily training continued but mainly to now test the bike and its set up and the results seemed acceptable. The gearing system was slick and its range was wide, although my configuration did reduce the number of gears that I could select on each front chain ring. This was expected as fitting 22-36-42 teethed rings in the front triple and a 11-36 cassette at the rear there was bound to be some chain slack and crossover clunking if I went down to a lower gear on that chain ring. I could take some links out of the chain but I allowed for this compromise as the more important higher gears could be selected without fail and probably would be used more anyway!

One safety device that turned out to be a lifesaver was a mirror, as a purist the fitting of a mirror on a bicycle should not have to happen but as we know an awareness of what is behind can make defensive riding more informed. Luckily I found a small mirror that slots neatly onto the STI brake hood under the rubber grip. This configuration kept the mirror high but out of the way of my hands. Strangely enough it worked better whilst fitted to the left STI when I was in the USA as opposed to the right STI for the UK?

The luggage on the bike consisted of two bright yellow *Ortlieb* panniers which clip onto the rear rack, a yellow 31 litre rack pack again by *Ortlieb* that cleverly fits on top of the rack and an *Ortlieb* bar bag on the handlebars that can take small items like cameras and phone. This bar bag as it contains my passport, tickets and money will accompany me everywhere for security, the other bags are locked to the bike using a loop lock.

This luggage set up I have used before as I prefer the weight when possible to be carried on the rear of the bike, I only use a front rack and panniers if carrying additional equipment such as when cycle camping. Having a light steering is preferable for me than the struggles and wobbles from a heavy unwieldy front end. The other decision to make would be what camera equipment to take to fully capture these amazing sights that I hope to cycle by. I know the iPhone has a good camera but was concerned that if this was damaged or lost all pictures and videos would also be lost.

The *GoPro* and handlebar mount would be great at capturing daily sights that I came across and a *Sony Cyber Shot* for stills, especially the Grand Canyon. To collate and provide regular updates to my blog/website was made easier by the *IPad Mini 4* with a card reader adaptor. So as soon as a micro or ordinary SD card were inserted it would transfer files to the *IPad minis* 128GB memory, for later transfer when a good internet connection was found to populate the *iPhoto's* cloud storage.

This was tested a few times to make sure that the concept worked and all appeared fine, the only drawback is that this bundle of gadgets and charging wires and spare booster battery weighed in at 3kg. Another heavy item which was not negotiable was the *Kryptonite Evolution Mini 5* D lock, fitted to its bracket on top of the rear rack between the saddle and rack bag. This was 1.5kg in weight but given that I may be stopping in some motels etc. that would not allow the bike in the room I had to make sure that the bike would still be there in the morning, a bit daft being on a bike ride with no bike! The tool kit although comprehensive, weighed in at a shade less than 2kg including two pumps.

The reason that I choose to take two pumps is during one of my previous bike rides in the Midlands, I had many punctures and whilst pumping the tyre back up after yet another repair the pump exploded. After pushing the bike four miles to a garage to pump it back up I promised myself that I would never ever be in that situation again, hence the belt and braces approach.

It all weighed in at 21kg for the bike in the disposable transit cardboard box and 17kg for the panniers and rack pack, these would satisfy the 23kg limit for *Virgin Atlantic*, the bar bag would become my carry-on bag. That was it, body and bike now made ready, tickets purchased, parking reserved for my transport selection of planes, trains and automobiles! Oh, and a ferry!

Chapter 4

Viva Las Vegas!

The *VW Polo* was all packed up with the bike and luggage and a flattened box in the back, beside my youngest daughter Chloe who kindly ensured that it stayed upright, although the front wheel did stick into her side most of the way. My wife Chris and I up front driving from Cornwall to Gatwick. An overnight stay in the *Premier Inn* and before I knew it I was checking in with *Virgin Atlantic* for the flight to Las Vegas together with 450 other transatlantic passengers. The boxed-up bike was accepted without any issues, it was now down to the baggage handlers to keep my trips dream alive.

After an emotional farewell to family at the airport, it was time to play the airport security game and see if my tray of possessions was cleared or not.

As I had foolishly not put my few disposable contact lenses in a clear plastic bag separately I was selected to have a drug swab on my bag. Once the result of "all clear" bonged from the drug sniffer machine I was allowed to continue on my way and to spend what felt like the next ½ mile circling left and right through the copious duty-free shops selling booze, fags, perfume and chocolates before I arrived eventually in the departures lounge. I thought tourist attractions were cruel to herd you out through their gift shops before tasting freedom, airports do it in reverse.

As I mentioned earlier I am not a good flyer, this probably stems from the many flights I took as a school kid flying from boarding school in the UK to Zambia (Africa) during every school holiday. Which perhaps does not sound scary unless you consider flying with *Zambia Airways* in the 1980's where on more than one occasion I visited countries that were on the flight path below us, as we landed often to carry out running repairs, refuel or just swap planes due to unforeseen circumstances i.e.to avoid a crash! The *Boeing 707*, although a good plane was past its sell by date in the 80's and was prone to breakdowns which is a worry at 38,000 feet. I recall being on the apron in Doula in West Africa during one rainy thunderstorm night and looking out the plane window at one of the engines being worked on as it had decided to expire and backfire (are these engines supposed to backfire?) 30 minutes and 3 miles up previously.

This engine was proving particularly troublesome; it had already necessitated us landing here, now the technician

with the hammer was punishing the petulant power plant!
The rest of that flight became very instrumental in my
subsequent life-long fear of flying.

This morning's flight was in a 17-year-old *Boeing 747*
which being superbly maintained by *Virgin Atlantic*
should do the trip in one go all being well. My seat was
upstairs in the 747's hump-so it felt like being in a
smaller plane and not a 450-seat behemoth.

Steve the passenger beside me was on a work trip
seminar to Vegas and he offered some suggestions on
casinos and attractions to visit in Vegas and as a regular
visitor to the US he also suggested not cycling at all
would be a great idea as well.

Then I watched lots of films, ate lots of food and had
some wine and drinks which all helped make the 10½
hours flight time move along nicely. Then at a local time
of mid-day we landed in Las Vegas, Nevada. My first
foray into the States was held up taking fingerprints and
a picture at passport control then at baggage collection
my bag containing the panniers came out record quick.

The bicycle cardboard box was not so fortunate. I could
not see an oversize collection point so asked one of the
staff; they explained it would come down the carousel
with the other baggage.

It won't fit I explained, oh then I am not sure where it
will go they replied. After asking about five different
people with a variety of answers and after all the
passengers had collected their bags I was left in the
baggage collection area on my own.

Eventually I heard a side door open and a box being
dragged by a determined baggage handler. I am sure he

must have dragged it by himself all the way from the plane. I thanked him profusely and told him he was my first American hero. Through customs on a wobbly trolley and then into the rather empty arrivals hall of the McCarran Las Vegas airport. I located an information desk and said that once I had built the bike I have a large cardboard box to dispose of and could they help? The reply was "yeah no problems". A nice quiet corner was found and in the oven like heat I went about building the bike, pumping up the tyres and clipping the panniers on. I had the occasional request from bystanders asking what on earth I was doing and in about 30 minutes I had made the bike ready and dropped off the unwanted cardboard box with the information help desk.

Now to start the ride, go out the building and head west to pick up a residential street to avoid the freeway. On my way out, I checked my plan with a police officer who was in his patrol car outside, he confirmed it was possible but still says "Good luck buddy- I still think you are mad".

The Las Vegas heat after the UK in April was intense and I only had a small bottle of water that I got from the plane, so I could not risk getting lost. GPS bike satellite navigation turned on and after about 5 minutes it realised it was in a different continent and adjusted itself accordingly, great news, if that had failed all my routes would have been worthless.

I hit the road and followed the pre-planned route although finding myself at a junction where the GPS said straight on but signs everywhere said left turn only, I suddenly became a pedestrian and used the crossing instead to get back on track. After a few miles, I hit the strip, with its six to eight lanes on each side full of both small mopeds to massive *Coca-Cola* trucks all vying for space on the metal studded surface of the road which had no marked or reserved lanes for bicycles, these were expected to tough it out with all the fast moving, horn hooting and exhaust belching impatient traffic.

I felt vulnerable and exposed in this maelstrom of fast vehicles with no safe-haven on the side of the road as a wall to protect the pedestrians blocked my access, I had to keep going until with fear the GPS said turn left.

This is frightening in the states as you must move over and position yourself in the correct lane hoping that some kind driver is aware of your troubles and allows you to move in front of them.

I made clear and excessive hand signals whilst looking back and trying to make eye contact with the driver to seek acceptance of my intentions but all the cars had blackened windows to the point that I could not personalise with anyone. This felt very uneasy and alien and downright scary. Then at the lights I notice that they do away with the amber before the green it just goes green straight from red and your off, although the lights seemed to stay red for a very, very long time compared to the UK.

Another concern at the lights is that traffic is permitted to turn right at a red light in the US, which stemmed from the oil crisis in the 1970's to save fuel, so as a cyclist you have to position yourself so that you do not impede any traffic that wants to turn right whist you are waiting to go straight on, after a while I found that cycling slowly towards a red light and moving faster when turned green was my best and safest bet. I was fully wired with the experiences before me and totally engrossed with both navigating and staying alive, the sights beyond the road were just a blur, an Eiffel tower here and a Statue of Liberty there were noted but ignored as I was looking for a pyramid.

Eventually an Egyptian Sphynx appeared on my right and then a black pyramid of the Luxor Hotel and Casino came into view as I rode into the limousine and valet covered parking entrance dwarfed by Egyptian God sculptures. I felt underdressed as a vehicle but still came to a well-earned celebratory stop and after dismounting the bike, pushed it into the world's largest atrium ready for check-in.

This went smoothly and as previously arranged the polite staff at the bell desk wheeled the bike into safe and secure storage for the next four nights allowing me to become a normal tourist and not a dirty smelly cyclist. The hotel was vast; inside this pyramid it was hollow so that you could look up the 30 floors and these floors are accessible via a sloping elevator to service the 4,400 bedrooms.

My room on the 24th floor was great and afforded views to the north, on the landing you could see right down the hollow pyramid to the theatres and food court below, on the floor below that was the casino, even at this height I could smell the cigarette smoke drifting up, Las Vegas was one of the few areas left that allowed smoking almost everywhere and as an ex-smoker of 15 years it smelt rank.

I unpacked the panniers, had a shower and decided to explore both the Luxor and the neighbouring Mandalay Bay casinos. The casinos are windowless hangers with injected calming aromas that contain machines with a multitude of flashing lights and annoying tunes based on themes from films, TV programmes and cartoons.

In the middle of most casinos are the tables where Blackjack, Craps and Roulette are played and fenced off is the high limits area, this is not an area I will visit. The players were a mix of ages and were either solo quiet players or noisy and brash large groups whooping and screaming at the turn of a card. Some people won and by the sound they were making it could be a big win but generally more money seemed to be going in than was coming out.

I had already set my limit of $60 maximum whilst in Las Vegas and only on a video poker machine playing Jacks or Better as the pay-out percentage was deemed higher, additionally you could play this a nickel at a time. As an unknown author wrote:" If you aim to leave Las Vegas with a small fortune, go there with a large one", I had neither so my gambling will be superbly dull. However, the smell of the fags drove me out before I could locate my chosen machine. I went outside for some fresh air in the desert heat which was a pleasant change and was chatting to some other tourists from the UK. Then I started the search for food and as a vegetarian this proved far more difficult than in the UK, eventually in *Rocket Burgers* I located a veggie burger which did the trick. Interestingly here is the States the soda drink is everlasting and you just keep helping yourself from the drinks machine, in the subsequent weeks to come this would allow me to drink vast quantities of fluids for a buck each.

The Deuce bus in Las Vegas costs $20 for 3 days unlimited use and is the best way to travel up and down the strip which is 5 miles long. So, armed with my mobile pass I set off north to downtown Las Vegas to visit the second highest observation tower in the Western world, the 1,150ft Stratosphere.

Yes, it was high, and the wind was brutal on the outside section, people were also riding a small attraction that rocked back and forth on the edge of the tower just stopping before they felt they were going to be thrown over.

All this mad fun continued as you could pay $120 to not use the lift and fall down the side of the tower at 40mph stopping just before the end. Not my idea of thrill seeking, the lift ride was more than enough excitement for me.

In the evening, I visited the Freemont Street Experience, which every hour shows a music video on the world's largest video screen located on the 90ft high curved ceiling running for 5 blocks and illuminated by

12.5 million LED's and to feel the performance a 550,000-watt sound system is used. It was impressive and awe-inspiring, especially as running underneath it every so often were people riding zip lines lying down four abreast screaming as they shot past. This was Vegas, brash, loud and in your face, you can win or lose a million dollars in a heartbeat, get married and divorced the same day- even have Elvis conduct the ceremony in a drive through chapel in a pink Cadillac.

You can visit a bar that is minus 20 degrees Celsius or a nightclub in a swimming pool or watch a hit Broadway show or an Elton John concert or fire a machine gun at a firing range or ride a helicopter along the strip-all there in Vegas. It's excessively wonderful and wonderfully excessive.

Going southbound on the Deuce bus through the brightly illuminated strip I stopped off at the Bellagio Hotel with its massive lake ready to watch the fountain show, the wait was not long as the programme starts every 15 minutes, my slot was Elton John's "Your Song" which had the 1,000 separate fountains dancing in time with the music in a hypnotic and memorable display culminating in a 500-foot high crescendo.

Impressed by the show I walked down the strip past the Elvis impersonators, the Can-Can girls, Superman talking to Spiderman and an assortment of very hot looking bears all willing to be photographed with you for five bucks.

Back on the bus I could see the Luxor hotel in the distance by the Sky Beam emanating from the top of the pyramid, this is the strongest beam of light in the world, in fact, aircraft at cruising altitudes can see it up to 275 miles away. In the dank ashtray smelling casino, back at the Luxor I succumbed to the heady lights and sounds and gambled $20 whilst enjoying two free drinks delivered by the very stressed waitress but unusually in Vegas I went to my room a winner as I was $50 up.

It was again early morning when I woke up, I say woke up but I had not been properly asleep as the 7 hours that I had lost due to the time zone was throwing my body clock into disarray, I hope that I can adjust to this soon, also disjointed was my appetite for not knowing if it was breakfast or dinner that I craved. Anyway, today I was off to Venice and Paris, albeit the Vegas abridged version.

After a short ride on the Deuce bus I found myself looking at a half-sized replica of the Eiffel tower. I went to the bottom of it into yet another casino that was created to look like a Parisian street complete with bistros and French police.

You could take a trip to the top or even have a meal in the tower but I have been up the real one and this one looked too neat and clean so I declined.

Close by in the Venetian Hotel and Casino you can stroll over a facsimile of the Rialto Bridge on its moving walkways looking down to the river with its Gondolas containing Gondoliers that sing to their passengers whilst rowing (I think just steering as they are electric) around the chlorinated pool water. They disappeared through a tunnel so I decided to see where they went, so after following the path inside and being whisked upwards on a curved escalator surrounded by marble statues and fountains I found myself on a busy shopping street with an artificial glossed black cobbled floor, although I was inside I looked up to a simulated blue sky with wisps of clouds in this synthetic hermetically sealed copy of Venice.

Around a few corners and the bright blue canal returned with its flotilla of Gondolas weaving in and out and under bridges masterfully steered by their singing skippers wearing striped shirts, red belts and straw hats to complete the illusion.

I left the building and found myself in St Mark's Square in Venice surrounded by noisy traffic whilst being exposed to the dry excessive desert heat. It was time for food so I stopped off at one of the many fast food restaurants to have a salad and coke and I must say that the customer care in the States is amazing and feels almost genuine in its approach. However, after hearing an American customer demean and shout at a member of staff over a trivial matter I can see that this relationship is very one sided, the staff member was then chastised by their employer and not protected from the abusive customer.

I think workers in the UK have more protection from over bearing customers which seems correct and morally right to me. I started to see the American dream in action, profit before people and people after profit- this seemed to be a fitting accolade, but I was here to observe and not to judge.

The following day I walked south on the strip to visit the Fabulous Las Vegas sign. Once I got to the sign in the middle of the road there was a queue or line as it's called in the States.

People were being professionally photographed in front of the sign wearing an assortment of costumes such as wedding dresses, cocktail dresses, even Elvis was there. We were surrounded by people selling tat or in the states they are called pan-handlers, I lose count how many people tried to sell me beers, drugs, water and tattoos, the last one seemed strange to me but it was Vegas after all. Just up from the sign is the Little Church of the West Wedding Chapel that was doing brisk business.

Then it was back up north to the New York, New York Casino. Outside is a scale model of the statue of liberty and the hotel building replicates the historic skyline of the buildings of 1940's New York City. Winding its way around them and into the building is a bright red track of the roller coaster that now includes VR (virtual reality) headsets for its riders so they can experience being on a roller coaster? Yes, I am confused by that one.

Inside the streets are replicating the borough of Brooklyn and have been fashioned with an eye to detail, even having steam rising from artificial drain covers. Outside I saw a cyclist, in fact a cyclist on an exact bike like mine, a British bike, although red in colour.

I had a chat with this fellow cyclist as you do and found out that Matthew was from Bristol and was a few weeks into crossing the entire USA on a bike after starting in San Francisco. He found himself in Las Vegas after being blown back by the strong 60mph headwinds that he had experienced.

He was here to meet up with his Brother who was flying over to meet up for a few days before he continued his ride. A very interesting and knowledgeable chap and he gave me some valuable insights and tips for my own cycling route as he had just returned from some of it, such as having 17 miles of a Freeway to myself thanks to on-going roadworks was great news.

We hoped to meet up in the Grand Canyon as it appeared that our paths might cross again there, in the meantime we exchanged numbers so we could check up on each other's progress.

He hopes to complete this mammoth ride on 21st June 2018 in New York- I wish him well and hope that his emergency welded bottom bracket holds out. I had one more day in Vegas before my ride started, I decided to fill up on calories so had another vegetarian burger and chips in the Rocket Burger, whilst waiting I was chatting to the cheerful staff member who explained she enjoyed working and living in Las Vegas but the desert heat in the hot months can reach 115 degrees Fahrenheit which is 46 degrees Celsius, remember this measurement is taken in the shade as well.

Today it was only 32 degrees and I was boiling. Afterwards I visited the medieval castle of Excalibur next door that had 4,000 rooms spread around a mock castle with turrets. Inside they have every night- knights jousting in a large arena whilst you have a hearty meal served on metal plates that you eat with your hands- medieval fashion whilst drinking mead out of a goblet. It was one of the first themed casinos in Vegas and proved to be popular.

I did read that they have also planned to build in the future a casino themed on the English, this Ye Oldie England casino would offer fish and chips, pie and mash surrounded by black cabs and red telephone boxes, one of the reasons behind this is that over half a million British tourists go to Las Vegas every year as part of the total 42 million annual Vegas visitors.

Departure day arrived being Thursday 19th April, I went to reception handed back my key and collected my bike from the bell desk, after checking all was complete I paid them a healthy tip of $20 which he refused at first until I explained how instrumental he was in my future quest. Bags loaded onto bike, camera mounted onto handlebars and three 1.5 litre water bottles stored in the rack pack for the expected heat. Farewell Las Vegas, it's been great but enough is enough, it's time to get back to the real world.

Chapter 5

Las Vegas to Boulder City via Hoover Dam

Today's journey was the ice breaker in the desert heat, leaving Las Vegas although scary was better than expected, I just went for it and followed my previously produced route hoping that it would avoid the worse junctions and busy traffic lanes. Leaving Las Vegas was always going to be uphill as it is in a large valley surrounded by hills. Fortunately, just outside Vegas I picked up a rare sight being an off-road cycle path in Henderson that wound its way up towards the hills and ran parallel with the interstate 515 through the railway pass at 2,500ft.

Here the interstate, railway and cycle path merged into a small slice through the hills and when I climbed over its crest the view it afforded me was amazing, I could literally see for miles down to Lake Mead to the north west and south to my destination tomorrow, it looked vast, barren and remote.

As I was stopping in Boulder City later I checked into the motel and dropped off my bags save for water and a toolkit in the now single pannier to reduce the weight to Hoover dam and back. The route had a long downhill section twisting left and right with signs warnings cyclists not to overtake other cyclists as a sharp bend was approaching on this paved off road cycle path alongside Highway 93.

I then picked up the Historic Railway Hiking Trail route that was created to transfer the materials to the dam site in the 1930's, this afforded a few miles of smallish climbs. The entrance gates warned that past this point without water was stupid and fatal, the trail turned to lose gravel so I am glad that I had shed around 15kg of luggage weight previously.

There were also signs that bighorn sheep were about on the rocks above me. The trail went through 6 massive tunnels that were driven through the rock and beside me below by a few hundred feet to the left was Lake Mead the largest man-made reservoir in the USA, created after damming the massive Colorado River. Before the trail ended I diverted off to the dam approach road into the public car park and locked the bike below a copious sized electricity pylon.

The path up to the highway 93 bridge was hot and steep but the view from the middle of the Mike O'Callaghan–Pat Tillman Memorial Bridge was incredible. This bridge with the largest concreate span bridge in the western world and nearly 1,000 feet above the gorge below was built a stone's throw from the dam. That dam is dam big I heard myself say and to think it was built back in the 1930's by thousands of men which cost 112 men their lives during construction. It is located on the border of Nevada and Arizona which also have separate time zones as well- so depending on the time of year you could lose or gain an hour walking across the bridge or dam.

After walking back to the bike, I continued freewheeling down the steep hairpin downhill road until the road went across the Hoover dam itself. Dismounting on the dam road in the dam middle and looking out over the dam wall the view looking back up to the Mike O'Callaghan–Pat Tillman Memorial Bridge was equally impressive as looking down. The ability of the engineers to build this dam in such a remote large gorge and anchor it against the adjoining sheer rock walls beggar's belief. Furthermore, to harness the Colorado rivers power and create hydroelectric electricity of 4 billion kilowatt-hours a year since 1939 is staggering.

A final fascinating fact is that the high scalers that used a wooden plank as a seat attached to a long rope and worked on the rock face were also showmen to visiting tourists who came to watch their death defying feats and one high scaler called Oliver Cowan saw his supervisor fall from the rock face above him, Cowan calmly caught his boss and saved him from a certain horrible death. Unfortunately, I was not confident enough to leave the bike for too long so did not do the dam tour around the inside of the dam and the turbine hall, which would have been dam interesting.

The route back was obviously a reverse of the way in but with the hills up all the way back to the motel and it was hot and exhausting thus I collapsed on the bed when back in the room of the Sands Motel.

Ride Data	
Date	19/4/18
Cycling Distance (Miles)	47.07
Cycling Time (Hours)	5:30
Average speed (mph)	7.8
Elevation Gain (feet)	4,039

Chapter 6

Boulder City to Searchlight

Next morning, I could feel the hills from yesterday, the dull ache in the thighs as if I had walked into the side of a table was ever present but the road was calling. I took a small detour to the post office to get some stamps for postcards as I had promised a family member that I would send a postcard back from each major place I visited. I went north to the junction of the main 93 freeway to go west and then to connect to the 95 going south to Searchlight.

At the first junction, it was just too busy to get over to the left turn lane and it was too early for my brain to be trusted. I once again became a pedestrian and used the crossing, patiently waiting for the white person signal at the other side, entertaining myself pressing the cross button that kept saying "wait" at every press. Whilst doing that a cyclist went the other way and shouted out "where you going?" to which I replied "Flagstaff", he carried on his journey.

Eventually I got to the correct side of the road and mounted the bike cycling along the very busy highway. Ten minutes later the same cyclist that I saw earlier rode up behind me, offering to help me with my puncture. I was a little confused but I soon learnt that when I had said Flagstaff he thought he heard "flat" and had turned around and chased after me.

This assistance being offered to me by a complete stranger is why I cycle, it allows you to see people naturally which is usually friendly, helpful and inquisitive. We stopped and had a long chat and he was called Al who had previously lived in the UK for 8 years and was now a Las Vegas resident and a keen cyclist, before we said our farewells I thanked him for looking out for me and he said he would follow my exploits on my web site. After a while I thankfully turned off the 93 to join the 95 at its start and moved over to the far right of the 10ft wide shoulder.

The views around me again were of a stark dry barren desert but with a massive solar farm glinting off to my right covering many acres stopping just short at the foot of the mountains that ringed around the entire horizon. Traffic levels were high with loads of trucks that have both a main body and a trailer behind which whipped past me doing at least 60-70mph, creating a vortex of high wind in its wake which both sucks and pushes the bike one after the other.

I learnt to ride these waves and I became adept of calculating the intensity and duration of these bow waves based on the size and speed of the truck coming up behind me. The wide road spread out ahead of me was razor straight and only disappeared into the far distance due to the heat haze that engulfed it.

The dry heat was becoming more intense and that forced me to stop more often to take drinks of water although it was now becoming mildly hot water. The lack of any shade was now worrying me as I could not see anywhere that I could take refuge under the scorching sun for a few minutes' respite. I had to endure the sun for my rides duration. The distance today of 42 miles was from a small city to a small town with nothing in between, no shop, garage, or even a tree to shade or rest at. My lunch today was made on the roadside using sliced bread and peanut butter; I ate this in the bright mid-day sun whilst being roasted like a peanut.

On the horizon after 35 miles I could see a large hill come into view; this was the town of Searchlight at 3,500 feet altitude, which was once a boom town after gold was discovered in 1907. It has since shrunk in size since all the gold has been mined out and now contains just a few stores, restaurants and a gas station and my time-warp motel called the El Rey.

The now repetitive daily processes of; checking into motel, having a shower, *Facetime* to home so they know I am still alive, finding meat free-food, updating the diary, transferring pictures from camera and GoPro were carried out. Once these have been accomplished it left the important body re-charge of at least 8 hours sleep, usually in maximum of 2 hour slots due to my body clock still being rather confused when and where I am.

Ride Data	
Date	20/4/18
Cycling Distance (Miles)	40.97
Cycling Time (Hours)	4:51
Average speed (mph)	8.4
Elevation Gain (feet)	2,180

Chapter 7

Searchlight to Laughlin

A night of little sleep due to the constant traffic noise was followed by an early morning start. I wheeled away from Searchlight looking at the disused slanted mineshaft lift towers that had previously provided so much wealth but were now just rusting monuments to times past. The road then started to roll downwards faster and faster which was great but then the road works signs appeared and stated that they would last for 17 miles.

This was another blow as the bollards forced me to the opposite carriageway which was the only side that was open to traffic. So, a complete freeway was squeezed into just 2 lanes with no shoulder. It was crazy, dangerous and to be honest it could not safely be endured for long whilst trying to stay alive, as trucks were passing within inches of my left arm making the bike shake violently. Over to the right I could see that the closed carriageway may possibly be able to handle a bike, it had no lines or studs but it had an asphalt surface.

Perhaps this was the road that Matthew had told me about previously, I decided for safety and sanity to give it a go; I pushed my bike over the rough road meridian and got onto the empty 2 lane carriageway. Its surface was superb and it was all mine and because it was the weekend I hoped that no workmen would be buzzing around the site either. For 17 miles, I was in heaven I could stop when I wanted; take any line on the road I desired as I had 2 lanes and a shoulder at my disposal. Every so often a bridge was being worked on and a bumpy narrow lane was my path across however I saw no workman on any of the road works and more importantly no traffic cops. As the sun got higher so did the temperature to the point that I am sure 35 degrees was exceeded. My only solution for this heat was my head protection scarf with flaps.

This Lawrence of Arabia contraption fits nicely under my bike helmet and it has flaps that cover my ears and neck to avoid sunburn, also when it gets too hot I drench it in water and it cools me down nicely when moving along. The heat rose as I continued downhill, the starting altitude was 3,500ft and Laughlin is at 500ft, so today is a luxury-all downhill. If you ever find yourself in the hot dry desert with a low humidity of about 10% be warned as your body starts to fail, in my case with constant nosebleeds and bleeding cracked lips, these were both painful and made me look like a bruised boxer.

All good things come to an end and the roadworks ceased, meaning I was back on the large shoulder of the fully restored freeway for the rest of the day. The road started to twist left and right whilst descending the gradient, warnings posted for trucks informing them of a down gradient for next 15 miles, were great news to me. The constant breeze of a 25mph downhill was cooling and refreshing and was one of the high points of the ride and it felt good, a touring bike can cross vast distances and is truly a remarkable invention and here I was crossing two states in the USA.

A left turn was now negotiated coming off the 95 to join the 163 east at Palm Gardens which wound its way through the mountain range dangerously close to the chasms at the side of the road, the only protection I had was a small 2ft barrier at the roadside. Once the rocky crests of the mountains were cleared an amazing view developed across the desert valley with the Colorado River separating Laughlin in Nevada and Bullhead City in Arizona in this valley basin of magnificent proportions.

Laughlin skyline in the far distance was impressive with its casinos and hotels hugging the Nevada riverbank, this resort oasis in the middle of the desert was created for satisfying the demand for gambling.

I continued down the hill towards this mecca of money not looking forward to gambling but an ice cold long drink that would be far more rewarding to me than any jackpot. I located the Tropicana Hotel and Casino and once again rolled up to the Limousine drop off zone. After locking the bike, I checked in with my minimal bright luggage and walked through to tower A of the resort.

On my way, you had to walk through the cacophony of the casino hall with the familiar noises and pungent odours. The room on the 4th floor was clean and large with a view South towards the Colorado Belle Paddle Steamer Hotel tied up on the riverside however, on closer inspection it is a normal building made to look like a paddle steamer-it's all part of the illusion.

I arranged for the bike to be looked after in the luggage store. Shortly afterwards in the smoky bar the ice-cold diet Pepsi was so refreshing that I thanked the barman with a tip. It must have been a sufficient amount as another Pepsi appeared which was downed equally as quick. I decided to take a walk around the area and was immediately hit with the heat when going outside. The walk along the riverside was popular and afforded views of the many jet skis and speedboats that were zipping up and down the Colorado river only being dissected by the many small ferries coming over from Arizona just a few hundred meters away.

I then came across a large car park that was full but only with hundreds of Corvette cars of all colours and opposite these were many stands selling Corvette related paraphernalia. A quick visit to the *In and Out Burger* and before I knew it I was sat munching through a beef-burger and chips which as a vegetarian was not easy but in my defence, I needed calories and quick and with no alternatives available I had to have protein in the form of meat.

I was losing too much weight and my energy levels were dangerously low and being aware that I had nearly 5,000 feet to climb tomorrow I needed fuel and fast. I polished off the burger with a hint of regret but I had already known previously that if needs must then meat would have to be eaten. At nightfall, I had another look around Laughlin which was still very warm and all the casinos were lit up in a variety of colours and even the paddle steamer casino had the paddles moving around and around with the effects of the neon lights.

On the way back to the hotel I saw the Nevada marijuana shop with a sign stating that if it's for medical use it costs 10% less than recreational use and it's grown locally, wow ethical and lower drug miles now.

Ride Data	
Date	21/4/18
Cycling Distance (Miles)	42.67
Cycling Time (Hours)	3:32
Average speed (mph)	12
Elevation Gain (feet)	966

Chapter 8

Laughlin to Kingman

A super early start today where I was on the road just before 6am, the hills ahead of me were best met before the expected 38 degrees. I joined Highway 68 which was another 4-lane freeway, fortunately with another wide shoulder to protect me and started my long 14 miles climb from 500ft to 3,600ft.

The gradient was high so that my speed was around 5-7mph on the climb and the road just kept going up and up. As a Cornish cyclist, I am fortunately used to hills but they do not go on for this long nor in this heat, truthfully I was struggling. I had 6 litres of water with me weighing me down in addition to my 17kg luggage and each pedal stroke was hard work.

I mentioned it earlier but fitness is a mind-set but my mind was both hurting and worried on the task before me. I pulled over and had a long drink, poured water over my scarf to cool myself down and had some trail mix (selection of nuts) and sat down listening to music to contemplate my negative approach.

Failure was not an option although I started to seriously doubt my abilities, I did a video diary, telephoned home and reviewed today's journey on the iPad. I now felt that I had expressed my fears to myself and my family, faced them and talked them away.

My mind-set had improved so I quickly got back on the bike, ensuring that I just looked at the view around me and not the many, many, miles ahead. I played a mind game with the stunning rocky outcrops around me trying to make out what nature was trying to sculpt and what object they reflected. Doing this I saw a hand, a throne and a half-eaten corn on the cob. Meanwhile the miles were being also eaten up, albeit rather slowly and then at the top of the hill looking out over the Golden Valley, which for 10 miles was almost flat and then before me was the straightest road I have ever seen; it was perfectly straight and only disappeared once it met the hills at the other end of the valley. It was an awesome sight.

I continued along the Golden Valley with a new-found lift in my mood, I was going to achieve todays target and not let the barren, dry, hot as an oven terrain get to me, I had now learnt to cocoon myself when required from all the negative influences around me and filter them out so all I could see and feel was the stunning natural beauty of my environment- I was in fact a lucky man, not a doomed man.

At the end of the valley I joined the 93 to start a slow climb up through the mountains again. Then a few miles on the 93 I saw lots of yellow jacket wearing people on the side of the road with bin bags galore. I pulled off at a gas station and treated myself to a cold Pepsi and an ice cream; I sat outside in the shaded seating area and chattered to the yellow jackets that were now all having a cold drink as well.

I found out that they belonged to a motorcycle group that had sponsored this part of the highway to keep it clean. This was sterling work as the state of the side of some of the roads I had seen were rather shameful and contained every sort of detritus you could imagine. I thought that this would be a good opportunity to confirm something that I had read about regarding rattlesnakes. I had seen them many times on the road thankfully in a squashed state and not rattling around. I questioned Steve the group snake expert with "Is it right that if I stomp and clap and make lots of noises it will frighten the rattlesnake and it will make it rattle thus revealing its location?" Steve replied with little emotion saying "rattlesnakes have now learnt to not rattle and will bite you without you ever knowing it was there!" Great news Steve, thanks for that, I wish I never asked.

The talk then got onto road safety and as motorcyclists they were more than aware of the dangers of not being seen by other drivers and as I was wearing a bright yellow jacket with "THINK BIKE" on the back I explained that in the UK a think bike educational strategy has been running for many years to try and address this issue for both motorcyclists and cyclist's safety. They all agreed a similar strategy in the States could make motorcycling a bit safer.

After they left to continue in their hard work I said hello to a chap who was looking over my bike and was asking questions about the set-up and my journey plan. This was the first time of many occasions where an American thought I was an Australian, I put him right and we discussed the issues of cycling in the USA. Back on the road and passing under the I40, it left Kingman just a few miles ahead, I was going to make it after all, now it seems strange, what was all the worry about 5 hours earlier?

The body heals quickly and I was feeling great although hungry. After checking into the booked motel, I popped out to my first ever visit of a Taco Bell restaurant and was surprised that there was a good selection of vegetarian food on offer, so a veggie Burrito and a salad was ordered. These turned out to be exceptional value and more importantly very tasty and very filling. I collapsed into bed around 10pm after watching a Star Wars film on the TV.

Ride Data	
Date	22/4/18
Cycling Distance (Miles)	38
Cycling Time (Hours)	6:00
Average speed (mph)	6.3
Elevation Gain (feet)	4,297

Chapter 9

Kingman to Peach Springs

Up early again and this motel provided an included continental breakfast of cereal and pastries which is great as it does help fuel you for the day and avoids the peanut butter and bread stops, which I can say is so bland, it's like eating asphalt covered with gravel. I avoided the coffee as I don't care much for it and went straight for the fruit juice but America runs on coffee and there was a nearly a mini riot when it ran out. I was looking forward to today's cycle as I would be riding the historic Route 66 all day.

The starting altitude was 3,500ft and over the next 46 miles I will climb to 4,800ft so a gentle climb all day and due to the elevation, I am hoping the heat will be less shocking than the last few days. Everything is set for a great day on the road and off I go, out of the motel and turn left onto route 66. Then as if on cue a flotilla of Harley Davidson motorbikes with leather clad middle aged men driving and females riding pillion went by in a deep resonating thud-thud noise so distinctive of the air-cooled Harley motorbike. Some riders waved at me, others nodded, either way they were all on their own pilgrimage to ride the 66 on a Hog.

This would be a common site whilst in Arizona and as an ex-motorbike rider myself I did have some jealousy towards their chosen form of transport, apart from many riders who chose only sunglasses as the protection for their head. Through bug gritted teeth they smiled, not a helmet in sight.

The Route 66 was a single lane road with a suitable side shoulder for me to ride on although pot-holed it was large enough to avoid the draft of the trucks passing me. This was great riding, not too hilly and the wind was behind me on a road that oozed history, crossing great desert high plains with the ever-present mountain range along the outside of this picture postcard countryside. Then the relative quiet was interrupted by the horn of the freight train approaching.

These are gigantic beasts that take up the entire horizon when chugging along, they may be slow but must be at least 2-3 miles long with their double height loaded containers being pulled along by at least 5 engines and a couple at the back for good measure.

As a kid, I used to watch goods train go past and hold my breath and see who could win first, do not try this in Arizona, you will expire long before the train goes past. I filmed one for my web site and the film lasted for 5 minutes. The road and train track were now inseparable moving up towards Peach Springs showing that these engines must be mighty powerful to pull trains up these gradients. I stopped off for a coke in Hackberry which has an historic gas station with a selection of old cars and petrol pumps outside and a gift store inside with Route 66 themed gifts aplenty. One part of the store was a museum in the form of a retro Route 66 diner complete with manikins dressed in the 50's styles and a glowing Wurlitzer juke box completing the scene.

Outside I spotted a reserved parking space for a Corvette but no Corvette; I had probably already seen it previously in the Corvette rally in Laughlin. Sitting in the shaded seating area outside having a cold coke was cool and relaxing and I got chatting to a couple riding a motorbike along this section of the 66 as an anniversary gift to each other, they were having great fun and after hearing my stories they agreed that their chosen method was an easier way to get their kicks, on Route 66.

As I climbed higher in the day trees started to appear around me, initially just a few then more and more were seen, this means that at least some shade was now available which is always a great comfort to a hot and bothered cyclist.

The steady almost hypnotic pedalling continued and my mind could enter the sweet spot of riding in the "grove", a head space that allows for a relaxed trance like state where no pain or worries can enter-this was cycling at its best and why I do it. Before I knew it Peach Springs was on the horizon, it had been a rather good days cycling. It was too early to check in so I spent some time cycling around this small Hualapai Indian reserve settlement, which consisted of a gas station, supermarket and a lodge hotel.

I went around the supermarket and got a coke and an ice cream and sat outside watching the school kids coming home from school from the local Indian reserve school. They were like school kids from anywhere in the world, loud and boisterous but when told to get out of the shop sternly they did so without any fuss or arguments, so perhaps not totally the same.

I could see the Hualapai lodge across the road and noted that it had a restaurant, as this was the only place for about 30 miles that I could eat I would visit there later. My room in the lodge was large and it was easy to accommodate the bike in the corner, surprisingly apart from the two casinos my bike has been allowed into every room so far. I did make a gaffe in reception when they said not to worry as they had a room for me and my bike on the first floor, so I responded with "I hope your lift is big enough to take my bike" they looked at me with a puzzled expression.

After a while I then realised my mistake as the first floor in the US is in fact our ground floor, so no lift is required-duh! Once I had explained my confusion I think they saw the funny side of it.

The restaurant was big and empty; I think that there were not too many guests currently staying at the lodge. The menu had lots of vegetarian choices which was another bonus and I had already seen that no alcohol is sold in this lodge due to it being on the Indian reservation. This I respected and had a cold coke which was perfect for me. The young waiter came over with a sheepish look and said that they were not running with their normal menu and had a stand-by menu for tonight and produced a typed A5 sheet of paper with a very slim menu choice.

I asked what vegetarian food they had to offer and his reply was a cheese and peperoni pizza. Oh, dear I thought, so I ordered a cheese pizza and fries and hold the peperoni. I crashed into bed watching Friends on TV, Phoebe found out she was having triplets, next thing I am gone, fast asleep, before I know it its 6am the following day.

Ride Data	
Date	23/4/18
Cycling Distance (Miles)	46.13
Cycling Time (Hours)	5:18
Average speed (mph)	8.7
Elevation Gain (feet)	1,819

Chapter 10

Peach Springs to Seligman

Breakfast was great as I helped myself to heaps and heaps of scrambled egg and toast and plenty of fruit juice hoping that this will keep me going until tonight as the road today looks quite bleak. I checked that I could take a few of the bananas from the display for later.

Strange but the restaurant was busy this morning with guests and it appeared that the majority were joining a lodge white-water rafting experience on the Colorado. I looked at a few of the pictures of this experience on the walls and it did look a bit sanitised over my own experiences of rafting.

The pictures showed all the passengers dry and in a double raft with a couple of outboard engines slung over the back whilst they went over a few rapids, all the time sitting comfortably. My experience of rafting was slightly more caveman in comparison.

It was back in 1992 on the river Zambezi which is the natural border between Zambia and Zimbabwe, both my brothers Dave and John and 6 others including the guide were in our raft. We each had a paddle and no foot holds so we had to balance sitting aside the rubber raft, and the trip lasted all day running through the Zambezi gorge. As we were paddling our success or failure was dependent on keeping the raft moving through the 25 or so rapids we traversed, most were class 4-5 and had names like *Morning Glory*, *Gnashing Jaws of Death* and *Washing Machine* and one class 6 called *Commercial Suicide* which we had to portage around as it was just too dangerous. On one nasty rapid we did flip onto the side of the raft and half the occupants fell out while I fell into the raft more by luck than design. Rafting… tried it and have the T shirt to prove it, no more rapids for me even on the Colorado River.

The roads today were straight and surrounded by high rocky topped hills each side and beside the road the desert floor was alive with Prairie Dogs which looked like a cross between a Meerkat and a Squirrel.
These were great fun to watch as they darted about and dived into their burrows. They were most confused what to do about seeing a bicycle I am sure they don't see many so they reacted differently each time.
There were hundreds of them around the roadside and when a car appeared they all barked like a squeaky toy and hid only to come slinking back out when the noise had passed. Unfortunately judging by the number

squashed on the road they did not always run the right way. These ex-Prairie Dogs now became food for the buzzards which swooped down and picked away at the flesh, only moving at the last minute when a car became dangerously close.

This is the beauty of cycle touring as all this activity would be missed in a car. The signs now stated that I was leaving the Hualapai Indian reserve and shortly I arrived at the tourist site of the Grand Canyon Caverns with an assortment of plastic dinosaurs positioned outside including a full-sized green T-rex. These dry caverns are 200ft deep and even have a restaurant at the bottom and the world's deepest hotel room where you are guaranteed a quiet night.

It was also a fully stocked fallout shelter during the Cuban missile crisis for up to 2,000 people and apparently, the supplies are still down there.

The name of Grand Canyon Caverns did seem a little deceptive as we were still some 120 miles from the Grand Canyon South Rim; I did read that some of the air in the caverns has made its way in from the Grand Canyon through fissures in the rock.

I went in to the shop in the museum and had a cold coke and whilst enjoying it outside I got chatting to a small group that were all going white water rafting, they were apprehensive so I tried to quell their fears by describing on my own previous rafting experiences, although I am not sure I helped much. There was also a gas station on the site that was designed to look like *Radiator Springs* version from the *Disney* film *Cars,* complete with a tractor, Lambretta and a rusty tow truck with two white goofy teeth to look like *Mater*.

Once back on the road I saw a pick-up in my mirror that was going slow and it then pulled up beside me, to which the women driver says "Howdy, there is a large load convoy coming up behind us and it would be great if I could pull over" the accent was different even to me and I think it was a strong Texan accent.

Anyway, I pulled over into the dirt and a massive lorry with police escort vehicles passed me by carrying an enormous orange construction bucket I assume for an excavator which was so wide it was taking up the entire road, the police officers clearly surprised at seeing a bicycle stopping for them all waved and thanked me for clearing the road. Then it was back to work peddling while making good steady progress towards Seligman which appeared around me by early afternoon. Seligman is a typical Route 66 town with many establishments to cater for the tourist. I was due to stop in the Supai Motel which had not changed much since Route 66 was the main road through these parts.

As I was early I went to a store and had the obligatory coke and ice cream to cool down whilst chatting to a woman who was telling me about Palmdale and Mojave as her husband works for Lockheed Martin who are based in Mojave, which I would be visiting in a few weeks' time. She also warned me about the hill towards Williams and the busy interstate 40, which I had to ride on in a few days' time as there is no alternative road. I checked into the Supai Motel and was chatting to the chilled manager who was enthusiastic about my ride, he showed me my room which although dated was clean and functional and with a hint of bygone times. Afterwards I walked up the road to the Road Runner café and gift shop and as I was ordering a meal the motel manager came in and arranged for me to have 10% discount off my bill as a motel guest.

I had a great meal, used their Wi-Fi and chatted to the saleswomen on the way out together with a Canadian couple who were equally engrossed in my exploits so far, although surrounded by Route 66 gifts all I could carry were a few postcards and some aluminium imitation number plates depicting Route 66, after all I had to keep my weight down.

Ride Data	
Date	24/4/18
Cycling Distance (Miles)	37.36
Cycling Time (Hours)	3:54
Average speed (mph)	9.6
Elevation Gain (feet)	1,308

Chapter 11

Seligman to Williams

Breakfast this morning was shared with a French family in the breakfast room which gave me an opportunity to use some of my limited French but it made the conversation much more limiting so we switched to English. The leg today was to be quite short, riding along Route 66 which runs parallel with the I40 until the last few miles which requires me to join this large road which is equivalent to a large UK motorway but cycling on it is allowed.

As the I40 is so close the only real traffic on the 66 was tourists in the shape of bikers and lots of recreational vehicles (RV's) soaking up the atmosphere and getting their own kicks on route 66.

Yet another advertising series by the *Burma-Shave* appeared on the side of the road, these have been popping up along Route 66 which has an unusual way of advertising its product. All the signs are burgundy in colour and about the size of a town name and the series consists of five signs with one every 300 yards or so. For example, one series was; *If you don't know,* gap, *Whose signs these are,* gap, *You haven't driven,* gap, *Very far!* gap, *Burma-Shave-the American safety razor.* Some also became very zen like, asking for people to fill out the blank signs with their imagination.

I always thought that advertising like this along a road was prohibited but clearly not in America; perhaps they pay for some sort of road maintenance. At my slow speed the message got lost on me but perhaps if you are travelling at 55mph they may make more sense hopefully, if you are not distracted by them, that could be why they were only found on the straight parts of the road.

The road now merged with the I40 and I found myself cycling along a large hard shoulder with trucks and cars once again whizzing past me at 70mph plus. The wide shoulder gave me a safe zone and as the sign requested when I joined I could only use the hard shoulder as a cyclist, not sure if any cyclists are stupid enough to start using lanes 1 or 2.

The shoulder also had a prominent rumble strip which consisted of groves cut into the top layer, so that if vehicles strayed over they would both hear and feel the rumble through the wheels. This helped me as I could hear if any vehicle approaching from behind was trespassing into my territory by the tyre rumble noise and I could dive into the dirt on the side if needed.

So, with ears, eyes and mirror working together I would hope to make it out alive from this unforgiving fast moving wackiest of wacky races. Then it was my turning to Ash Fork which I took, glad to be away from the constant noise and I entered the sleepy town, now ignored as bypassed within yards of the I40.

The small town had a large one way system which seemed pointless having a one way road going around essentially a ghost town. I stopped at the post office to post my latest postcard to the UK. Then I pulled over and had a cold coke from the gas station and I could see my motel just around the corner, however I had an epiphany. If I carried on to Williams today it would allow me a rest day tomorrow as I would be a day ahead of myself, this would allow my body a day to rest and I could spend some time looking at the sights in the historic town of Williams. I looked on *Booking.com* to check that I could book an additional night in Williams and that my hotel in Ash Fork could be cancelled free of charge.

Both were possible so I quickly re-arranged my bookings and prepared myself for a long afternoon on the I40 and the Olympic climb from 3,400ft to 7,000ft over 18 miles. It seemed to me that the conditions on the I40 were manageable and the heat tolerable so time to saddle up and go for it.

Just after I entered the I40 the road works sign stated these were in place for the next 35 miles, followed by shoulder is closed ahead sign. Uh oh, this is not what I wanted but with no alternative road available I had to continue onwards.

The right lane was closed by bollards but I could slip behind them and stay on the far right-hand side which as it turned out made for a very safe cycling experience. The single traffic lane that was left was not able to handle all the traffic going up the long hill and a traffic jam formed which snaked its way slowly up the hill.

The gradient made the hill hard work, however I could stop at any point which I often did to have a drink of the now warm water that I was carrying.

Around me on the parched hillside were many small isolated ranches with either horses or cattle or both, they must have been sweltering in the heat. The terrain was also changing as the trees started to grow taller and taller the higher I went and I started to spot some distinctive

Ponderosa trees amongst them. At last the hill came to an end and I arrived on the outskirts of Williams, I took the junction and there before me was the Days Inn motel, it would be my base for 2 nights, time to recharge, do some laundry and generally chill out.

I also saw a wild west show down by the railway station in the morning, where there was a lot of shooting, gun smoke and cussing, the marshal being the goodie won the day. Then I had lunch over by Cataract Lake which was visually stunning, set amongst the mountains and thick forest, whilst at the same time watching a brave inquisitive family of deer who decided to come over and stay with me for a while.

Ride Data	
Date	25/4/18
Cycling Distance (Miles)	48.21
Cycling Time (Hours)	5:51
Average speed (mph)	7.6
Elevation Gain (feet)	3,149

Chapter 12

Williams to Valle

The rest day was beneficial to the body and to get everything sorted out such as re-packing the panniers to get most of the weight closest to the rear spindle. This would make the handling more precise and hopefully less wobbly. After having breakfast complete with mounds of scrambled egg and toast it was time to put it to the test.

I now bid farewell to Route 66 and will see just a short section of it again in a few days' time when in Flagstaff. I now join the highway 64 going north towards the south rim of the Grand Canyon to my stop in the town of Valle. The road has a small shoulder but it had massive potholes so I had to keep darting out into the road in a form of cycling Russian roulette.

As this is the main road to the Grand Canyon it was quite stuffed full of coaches, cars and RV's and as there were a lot of road works taking place in Grand Canyon village there were also stacks of construction trucks to add into the mix.

At 10am the Williams to Grand Canyon tourist train went past complete with its glinting glass observation dome roof to give those lucky passengers an even finer view of the massive plateau around us, interrupted only with a few massive rocky outcrops rising a few thousand feet higher.

Knowing that north of me was the Earths biggest canyon was exciting and I found it strange that there were no clues around me of this in the current terrain. I then got thinking of the early pioneers who could have come this way to make a new life in the west, travelling by horse and cart with all their belongings and all their family, taking a week to traverse the visible horizon that I could cover in a day on a smooth road. Then they would have the Grand Canyon block their way- what would go through their minds? Go around? But its 250 miles wide! This is a true pioneering spirit that I have identified as the character within the American people.

The road went on and on over long downs and short ups like some gigantic roller coaster trying to get faster and faster, for me it is satisfying to use my speed from the downhills to help get up some of the uphill.

Then I saw the *Yabba Dabba Doo* sign in the distance, this must be Valle with the *Flintstones Bedrock City* tourist attraction. Then on the left I saw the Planes of Fame aircraft museum which I had planned to visit, so I pushed my bike to the window of the office, put it on its stand and went in.

The curator said he would keep an eye on the bike although he said that not many people frequent this area. I paid $10 to get in and walked around the fascinating indoor collections of historic aircraft complete with interesting real-life stories.

Some of the aircraft are also so well maintained that they fly them occasionally so that they are not just static but flying museum pieces.

About a mile up the road was the Grand Canyon Inn and Motel, my pre-booked motel. As I was too early to check in I went to the restaurant come bar and had a Grand Canyon Brewery beer to cool down, in fact this was my first local American beer which was brewed back in

Williams, perhaps the lowest beer miles I could have chosen and it tasted great.

After an age, I could check-in and then got a key for a room in an annex of rooms across the road. Once I got over the other side there were a collection of small chalets which although very, very small were once again suitable for one night for a cyclist, not sure if the other guests would be so accepting of the Wendy house dimensions.

I nipped out for food and on the way back I noted an Indian gift shop called the Double Eagle Trading Post, I went in and saw a couple of small light items that were suitable gifts and waited at the till to pay.

The shop was completely empty of any people apart from me, so I tapped, coughed, knocked, shouted, walked noisily around but it was devoid of any staff. I checked the door to make sure it was signed as open and yes it was.

After a long time, someone appeared after hearing one of my additional shouts of "shop".

He was very apologetic and he explained that he has an office out back and listens for cars on the gravel car park, the fact I walked was alien in the US. I squeezed back into the motel chalet and had to put the heating on as it got a bit chilly in the evening.

Ride Data	
Date	27/4/18
Cycling Distance (Miles)	32.67
Cycling Time (Hours)	3:00
Average speed (mph)	10.8
Elevation Gain (feet)	649

Chapter 13

Valle to Grand Canyon South Rim

I am going to see the Grand Canyon today I thought to myself, I can tick off two of the seven natural wonders of the world. I had already seen Victoria Falls in Africa twice and that was an amazing sight that stays like an imprint on your mind due to its absolute beauty.

I just need to cycle 40 miles and I will be staring over one of the many vantage viewpoints, also I had arranged to *Facetime* with my family if a signal was available so they could share the moment with me, wow modern technology. Back on the road again, whilst being particularly cautious as the number of tourist coaches heading my way was increasing and they did not give anywhere near the 3ft legal minimum distance passing a bicycle, I think they misread it to 3 inches.

After a few hours, I cycled into Tusayan which had a large selection of hotels and fast food restaurants; I headed straight for the visitor centre as I needed a pass to enter the Grand Canyon National Park, which as a cyclist was $15, which lasts a week.

As a method to try and reduce the mile-long queues or "lines" that form during busy times the park authorities have created a cycle path or "greenway" leading through the Kaibab natural forest.

I joined this outside the visitor centre and was relieved to see it was paved and so for the next 15 miles I had a most relaxing off road ride through the shaded forest. Strangely enough I only saw four other cyclists on this very expensive white elephant of a greenway, I thought, good luck getting people out of their cars that's all I can say. The path went up and down, it went left and right, in any direction that was not the most direct but I was away from the traffic so mustn't grumble. I then arrived in a large car park and the trail abruptly stopped, so I headed north to the main lookout and judging by the number of people around it must be the right area.

Then I saw it, the Grand Canyon in real time, this is where words, pictures or videos cannot do it justice as the scale, depth and colours are beyond anything that we can use to describe or record it.

Its vastness was what hit me the most, I could use superlatives all day long but once again it would not allow you the reader to fully appreciate what is in front of my eyes. You are going to have to take my word for it and listening to the comments of my fellow awe-inspired onlookers they were having the same difficulty taking it all in as well.

I got a phone signal and used *Facetime* to talk to the family who were impressed with the video they were seeing even if it was just a fraction of the quality of real-life. I just stood there looking around and feeling so very insignificant in all of it, it was the first time that I got emotional over a view, it was astounding.

As I walked down the rim path to the various other vantage points the view was different but equally amazing. In the distance, I could see the mighty Colorado River which was the cause of this massive 1,800-million-year-old canyon which at 1 mile deep and 277 miles long, with an average width of 10 miles and at an elevation of 7-8,000 feet sure made for one big hole. The trail southwards took me past some rim-side hotels with luxury rooms overlooking the canyon with prices to reflect. Around the Grand Canyon Village virtually every road was dug up and a bumpy gravel thoroughfare was all that was left, instead of doing the road in sections they were doing it all at the same time, this made cycling dangerous and uncomfortable.

At Bright Angel, the automatic barrier across the road blocked all traffic apart from the free bus service from entering Hermit road but cycling was permitted. I cycled up the steep hill towards Mohave Point all the time aware that the Canyon on my right was not too far from the road and every so often I glimpsed the stunning scenery and was drawn to stop at every vantage point there was.

At Mohave Point, there were less tourists and more hikers as this was about 5 miles away from the main village, as it was quieter I set up the GoPro to take some 4K films and photos in a vain attempt to capture greater detail, although I expect that 14K would be required to do it justice, if such a resolution existed.

At one point, I saw a helicopter fly through the canyon below me and it was being dwarfed by the sides of the canyon walls. About an hour later I managed to pull myself away to return to the village to find the Maswik Lodge, tonight's overnight stay.

The room was in a separate building away from reception and the self-service food hall and was on the 2nd floor with no lift available. Lugging the bike up the outside stairs was tough but necessary, it avoided locking the bike outside and carrying all the panniers up the stairs, this way it was just one largish item to manhandle and not lots of separate bags. The room provided was massive as it had two double beds, so there was plenty of room for the bike.

No air-con was fitted in the room but the temperature felt fine; anyways I could always open a window. After a shower, I grabbed some food in the self-service restaurant and low and behold a vegetarian menu of chilli con carne followed by lemon meringue dessert all for $10, not bad. It is a tradition in the Grand Canyon that you try to watch at least one sun-set, so I walked over to the rim and sat watching the sun start its descent with many other spectators and we were not disappointed.

As the sun started to set, areas of the canyon became more visible and some were creating lengthening shadows behind them, the entire vista was changing before our very eyes. What had been hidden in the shadows became bright and luminesced in all its glory as if knowing this would be short lived blaze due to the suns rapid journey west.

The sun set behind the horizon and darkness was taking over; at the same time, it got jolly cold, jolly quick, so a rapid walk along the rim to the lodge helped me to warm up. In the room, I had so many pictures and videos to transfer to the iPad, it could not all be done that night and as it transpired it would take another week for these to be uploaded to the cloud storage, even when I had a very good Wi-Fi connection. I also noted that my small tube of *Pringles* crisps was more than ready to pop, as at 7,200ft altitude any air in sealed containers expands to the point that my Pringles did not pop but explode when opened.

It was now late and I tried to get some sleep but here more than anywhere one of the annoying things about America was determined to keep me awake, in the car park below there was a lot of coming and goings but that was not the problem, the issue is when you remote lock a car over here the horn hoots twice loudly and it does the same when its unlocked.

I am not sure how the Americans tolerate this constant hooting both night and day, I just hope that this trend does not come across the pond to the UK, its infuriating-be warned.

Ride Data	
Date	28/4/18
Cycling Distance (Miles)	36.38
Cycling Time (Hours)	4:32
Average speed (mph)	8
Elevation Gain (feet)	2,731

Chapter 14

Grand Canyon South Rim to Cameron

Knowing that it is more downhill than uphill today was a great feeling to have when I woke up. Add to that seeing the canyon beside me for most of my 60-mile ride was a double reason to get up and ready for the day. After bouncing my fully-laden bike down the stairs, I joined the rim road heading east and was immediately nearly run off the road by a bad batch of cars eager to pass each other and exceed the posted 35mph limit in the National Park.

After a few miles, I pulled over to look across the canyon and as it was still early not many other spectators were about. Same canyon but a totally different view was before me and a totally stunning panorama that deserved many more pictures, I am so glad digital cameras allow you to photograph everything hundreds of times as someone who remembers and used 35mm film and the restrictions it placed on the photographer and their budget.

I continued enjoying the view immensely I just wished they drove on the left as I would be right next to the rim instead I had a lane in my way.

The wind started to blow hard as I noted we were at 7,500ft and the news had given a wind advisory warning this morning, just make sure that I do not go too close to the edge of the canyon taking pictures etc. as a strong gust of wind has been known to blow unsuspecting spectators into the abyss, I don't want to be another statistic.

To my right was the Kaibab natural forest that was alive with creatures scurrying around in the undergrowth which turned out to be squirrels and once again a few had got too close to the road and ended up littering the roadside.

At Navajo point I looked across the void and on the escarpment opposite sat the 70ft high Desert View Watchtower perched aside the edge of the cliff. I could also see more of the Colorado River today and it was strange to see the green vegetation sliver that grew beside the river as it went downstream when all around was barren parched red, orange and brown rocks.

A short cycle later I stopped off at the watchtower and climbed up to the roof observation level where the view was spectacular once again.

On one side was a sudden drop of about 2,000 feet straight down into the ravine below, once again the magnitude of size was massive all around me. A quick look around the gift shop where unfortunately most items were large and/or heavy so just a few postcards this time. Up the path I popped into the café for a berry smoothie which although sharp was tasty.

Outside I met a couple called Stu and Barb who were travelling around the USA writing a video blog, we got chatting and Barb asked if she could interview an Englishman on his cycle travels. No worries I thought, so in the wind I explained why I was there and where I am going and she asked me to demonstrate the GPS as well. I bid farewell to them both and have since been following their travels which has been fascinating and extensive. A few days later I saw the video on YouTube and it was very good even if I was the star, roll on Hollywood. Around ten miles later the Grand Canyon lost some of its grand and was becoming decidedly less hilly as I travelled east as the main canyon has turned north, the smaller canyon containing the Little Colorado River stayed beside me.

The wind picked up to become very gusty on my left side, sometimes threatening to push me over the small roadside barriers into the gorge beside me, added to that the gradient downhill was becoming steeper and steeper and the shoulder was getting narrower and narrower.

I was getting faster and faster going down the extensive hill, whilst leaning the bike to try and compensate for the side-wind and trying to maintain a safe line around the steep corners whilst at the same time making sure that nothing behind was trying to overtake me with traffic coming the other way.

It was all rather exhilarating, I tried to keep the speed no faster than 35-40mph as I thought I had some element of control up to that speed, I do not know what this assumption is based on however as it's not something you would want to consciously test.

Then the tell-tale acrid smell of hot molten brake-blocks filled the air, I pulled over to check the rim temperatures and I burnt my fingers on them. Oops they are running a little hot, time to stop, rest and let them cool down or risk an explosive over pressure tyre blow-out. I had to repeat this quite a few times down that 3,500ft descent over 30 miles.

Then the heat returned into the air as I had reduced my altitude going from around 25 degrees to over 33 degrees in the last 10 miles. Once again my water supply was warming up to meet the ambient temperature, should have brought some tea bags with me for a brew. I put my sun-scarf garment on to protect my head, neck and ears from getting burnt and used some of my warm water to soak the material as when moving along this was superb at cooling the head.

Luckily I had already established a routine every morning to apply factor 30 sun-block oil so had not experienced any serious sunburn yet and hoped to keep it that way. I suddenly noticed that the time on my GPS went back an hour, I was confused, what's going on I thought? I checked my phone and that had also lost an hour as well, so this is what the twilight zone looks like as I couldn't think of a rational answer.

Then it was the end of the line for route 64 as I joined the 89 being the main road serving Tuba City in the north to Flagstaff in the south so it became a lot busier.

Now I had to do one thing that I hate whilst cycle touring and that is to go down a road that I will need to double back on in the morning, adding around 4 miles onto the journey but it could not be helped as the Cameron Trading Post was the only motel around for many miles. After negotiating the rare roundabout where everyone was totally confused what to do I arrived at the motel. The first thing I did was look at the massive clock behind reception and that was an hour ahead of all my timepieces, what the *$&* is going on! So, I asked the helpful receptionist what was the issue with time around here not being a constant? The answer was straightforward; the Indian reserve of Navajo which I entered 10 miles ago observes daylight savings hour whereas the state of Arizona does not, which is why at this time of year Arizona and Nevada have the same time, although they are in different time zones.

The motel chose to keep its time synchronised with the rest of Arizona or all its guests would arrive early and leave late and be confused in the process and I don't know if I got that the right way around because I get muddled just thinking about it.

As I had not arrived an hour earlier I was now not early and able to check-in within the early period! The room was in another block and was on the 2nd floor, no worries- I've got this, as I bundled the loaded bike up the stairs along the corridor to the room which once again was massive and decorated in a very pleasant strong Indian style.

A great view out front of the room took in the lower part of the canyon with the now closed old suspension bridge across the Little Colorado River gorge. I then saw the clock on the bedside cabinet and started to worry what time to set my alarm for the morning, in fact I had to call home for advice as I could not work it out-what a doughnut. After a quick shower, I went to the restaurant and had a veggie burger and fries whilst having a chat with the efficient waiter called Simon. It turns out that most of the staff in the motel share-own the business so all contribute to its day to day running, a bit like a cooperative.

We also talked about the concept of tipping which I explained was rare in the UK apart from in restaurants. He was confused as he was unsure how staff who serve people in the UK survived without tips, here in the USA it is accepted that 15-20% of your total bill for a meal is given as a tip to your serving staff, a taxi would be 10-15%, even buying a beer in a bar you should hand a buck to the barman, everyone gets a tip without fail obviously based on the service received. I replied that tipping in the UK although not compulsory did exist in a few areas, although the employer was responsible to pay a suitable salary to their employees so that tips were a wage bonus and not just required to make the wages tolerable i.e. not subsidising an employer.

I added that tipping in Japan is regarded as an insult, so every country has their own system I suppose. After the meal, I made sure to add 20% tip considering our previous conversation and of course the excellent service received.

Ride Data	
Date	29/4/18
Cycling Distance (Miles)	58.8
Cycling Time (Hours)	5:33
Average speed (mph)	10.6
Elevation Gain (feet)	2,488

Chapter 15

Cameron to Flagstaff then Amtrak to Los Angeles

As said before I do not like re-tracing my steps but I had to this morning, so I broke the journey by stopping for a pancake breakfast at Mc Donald's with an iced coffee, not something I would have very often but todays climb totalling 3,600ft means I need energy. Also, todays ride had nowhere to stop for supplies so it was 55 miles of bleakness without a store, what I needed had to be carried with me.

Flagstaff is located due south of me and is 10 miles behind the biggest mountain in the area called Humphrey's Peak standing at 12,633 feet, I could see the snow-capped peaks in the far distance in the range of mountains called the Kachina Peaks Wilderness so, for once I had a visual reminder of the distance to cover during the second half of the ride. I was repaid the lost hour which was borrowed from me at around 10 miles outside Cameron so the status quo was now returned. I once again got into the 'grove" and piled through the miles and the hours, I did stop once when something glinted at the side of the road.

I had already decided that if I found any licence plates on the side of the road I would take them home as a souvenir as they are light, original and I am doing my bit for recycling, anyway this glint turned out to be a bent New York plate and was the first in my collection which grew over the next few weeks. The uphill struggle continued unrelenting with the systematic turning of the pedals with feet clicked in to the cleats to maintain only around 5mph hour after hour. Then at 7,290ft the climbing stopped and it was downhill from here into Flagstaff but it sure was cold going down that hill but it meant I had broken the day's ride and will meet the train to Los Angeles. Flagstaff was big and after being in the desert it was strange to be back in lines of traffic having to fight for position.

I followed the train track into the centre and then to the university and as I had seven hours before tonight's Amtrak I had booked a Travelodge although not staying in it all night it allows me to have a shower and help prepare the bike and luggage for the next stage of my journey being the transit of California. So, at 8pm I returned to reception and handed the keys back which was met with some confusion but after explaining that I had a train to catch it made sense to them.

A short ride to Flagstaff station and when I arrived both my panniers and rack pack were put into a collapsible bag that I had used on the flight over from the UK, so this reduced my luggage to just one bag, this I checked in as luggage with the Amtrak office to make my journey easier. I just had to concentrate on getting the bike to the baggage car when the train arrived. In the Flagstaff waiting room I detected an English accent and not only that he arrived by bicycle, turned out that Daniel moved to the States when his parents emigrated to Phoenix five years ago.

He now worked as a cardiac nurse in Long Beach and was returning from a mountain bike competition in Williams. Respect to him as he had cycled from Williams on a mountain bike using the most direct route being the busy interstate 40. We had a good chat about many aspects of American lives and one area that I knew little about was the health care system.

He explained that insurance details were just as important as your name and medical history as this would impact what you need to pay in any excess amounts usually in the thousands of dollars. Medicare is available for over 65 year olds but before that health insurance for a family could cost around $1,500 per month, also coverage for pre-existing conditions could reduce your cover. If you don't have insurance, then the level of your medical intervention could be affected.

In the UK where healthcare is free at entry under the NHS system as it is funded via taxation, these American arrangements do seem strange and somewhat competitive.

Healthcare for profit just seems a contradiction to me but what do I know. Daniel did go on to tell me that there is a heart disease epidemic in America that is getting worse every year.

Eventually, the train turned up 40 minutes late which was the norm I had been told and we were asked to take our bikes to the baggage car which was at the front of the train, so we legged it down to the other end of the platform as Daniel had told me that they don't hang around for long.

We got to the baggage car and handed our bikes up 5 foot in the air to reach the doorway, I told him that we are going to Union Station in LA. Nothing was handed back in return and I was not expecting anything either- the person we had checked in with the Flagstaff office was also there handing over our checked bags, so it seemed reasonable to me that my checked bag receipt would also cover the bike. Then it was time to sprint back to the rear of the train to get back to the standard class coaches as it was only the first and sleeper carriages that were at this end, curiously enough you are unable to go through the train to get to the rear either. I am just glad the passenger trains are not as gigantic as the freight trains for obvious reasons.

Both Daniel and myself showed our tickets and Daniel helped me locate the correct seating area upstairs as I was after all an Amtrak newbie. As it was relatively quiet and an overnight train Daniel and I found separate available double seats, I bid him farewell until LA and I settled down in the most enormous seat on a train I have ever encountered, it was humungous, with adjustable footrests and adjustable leg rests and a reclining seat as well. However, it was designed for a larger person than me and try as I might with adjusting this and that I just could not get comfortable, give me a British Rail seat any day, I used to sleep on those sitting bolt upright as my body adjusted to the seat, I am not used or accustomed for the seat to adjust to my body it just does not work. The train was super slow as the distance is around 400 miles to LA and it was going to take 12 hours so that's an average speed of approx. 35mph.

The train rocked back and forth violently the faster we went and the noise from the wheels on the rails was alarming, will it make it I thought. Looking out the windows some familiar places came into view through the night such as Williams, Seligman, Peach Springs,

Kingman and Laughlin it was so strange to start seeing these places in reverse. I think that I achieved about an hour's sleep on the swaying shaking train.

I was very groggy when we arrived in Union Station Los Angeles. I met up with Daniel and we started along the platform to the front of the train to collect our bikes.

At the baggage car, the same baggage handler we spoke to in Flagstaff was emptying the checked luggage onto a flatbed truck; he recognised us and started to get our bikes but then his colleague asked for our baggage tags. What tags? I said, so I showed him my checked bag tag to which he responded "that's for your checked bag collection, it's not a bike tag".

Daniel was getting frustrated and started to lose his temper. The *Amtrak* luggage staff member who I shall now refer to as Mr Jobsworth said "you need to go to the office and explain the situation; I can't give you your bikes". I exclaimed being as calm as can be with "My bike is a green Dawes Galaxy with drop handlebars and a black Brooks saddle, can you please check it's still there as I would hate to find out that you have returned it to someone posing as me prior to LA". He went away down the baggage car for a while and returned with my bike which he just handed down to me without saying anything-just a nod, "cheers mate" I said, result I thought, so I told Daniel to do the same thing but he just lost it and turned a stressful situation into a battle of wills.

I wished Daniel luck and said cheerio to him and hoped that his bike situation would soon be resolved but I had to go and collect my checked bag for which this time I had a tag for. Union station is a typical large American station with Art Deco styling and a large central hall with a wooden high ceiling. The checked baggage collection area was in the corner behind *Starbucks*, I could see my bag on the small carousel so after showing the handlers my tag it was handed to me. 5 Minutes later all the panniers were re-attached to the rear of the bike and the collapsible bag was collapsed and stowed. Next, I wheeled over to the toilets and found a large cubicle equipped with a sink to get changed into my cycling attire, have a wash, put in contact lenses and I was ready to face the traffic of Los Angeles, ready or not.

Ride Data	
Date	30/4/18
Cycling Distance (Miles)	53.68
Cycling Time (Hours)	7:47
Average speed (mph)	6.9
Elevation Gain (feet)	3,622

Chapter 16

LA circuits to Culver City

"Wait" the crossing said, next press, "Wait" another robotic reply, about an age later the white person signal appeared so I crossed over, saw the cycle path beside the road and started to cycle on one massive urban sprawl, in fact even more spread out than London.

My route was to head south to Long Beach and then head across to Palos Verdes- around 45 miles with hardly any climbs.

The cycle paths were nice and bright green here, also cars were encouraged only to merge across if turning right on the broken green spaces on the road and overall it seemed to be accepted and work most of the time. It was deceptively easy cycling presently and the miles rolled by until the cycle path disappeared and was replaced with a painted picture of a bike stencilled on the road with double arrows above it like a sergeant's stripes. This small difference resulted in an evident change in driver's behaviour as close passes, right hooks and beeping from behind became the habitual practice.

This was to be repeated as I cycled through different council districts that had different views on cycle safety with facilities ranging from zilch to bright green cycle lanes and bike only paths equipped with bike only traffic lights. Oh, I dream of joined up thinking by council planners. Also, why do they put cycle routes along industrial estates with their large trucks constantly moving around? Seems daft and needlessly dangerous to me.

The city went on and on, sometimes retail areas and sometimes residential, some poor neighbourhoods and some very rich neighbourhoods, they all went by.

The most striking neighbourhoods were the tent cities that sprang up under freeway bridges and beside disused land.

These areas were busy with people who clearly had little possessions and no sanitary facilities either. I was in the richest and most powerful nation on Earth and was seeing first hand that the American dream is in fact a nightmare to some of its residents.

I am aware of the homeless problem in the UK as I used to run a homeless charity in London during the end of the 1980's, which was at the height of the Thatcher government's privatisation strategy and the start of the care in the community ethos.

I witnessed first hand the despair, poverty and isolation that occurred if you could not for any reason provide for yourself or your family be it through illness, disability or just bad luck. The situation in London did improve slightly over the 1990's with funding, compassion and resources, as it was a national scandal and not just a London issue. However, homelessness is still a major issue in the UK with over 1.5 million people and families on the social housing waiting lists currently, as there is just too little housing stock available.

I am not sure that the tent city before me and the many others that I would come across in my USA travels will only be a temporary solution to their housing crisis; I hope and pray that human compassion will soon step in and improve their lot. I joined up with the Los Angeles River as the cycle path ran alongside; this will take me down close to Long Beach on the south of the city.

The river here is wide and unlike our rivers it is surrounded by a concreate sleeve on its walls and floor, I assume to allow it to flow fast when required to avoid floods. It only had the smallest stream in the middle but the channel was both wide and deep in preparation for subsequent massive flows. Under all the bridges more tent habitats were established being just a stone's throw away from exclusive properties that also lined the riverbank. Cycling was good as the path was wide and well maintained as it also doubled as the access road to the river for maintenance and it was totally flat.

Ahead of me I could see the cranes on the right which marked the Terminal Island freight port which Daniel had warned me was not an area to cycle around due to the number of heavy truck movements.

The path now directed me across a bridge over the Queensway Bay and half way across I could see the 1934 Clydebank built RMS Queen Mary moored alongside the quay, since 1967 it has been a hotel and museum. I cycled over to the quayside beside the Scottish ship and looked up at the splendid vessel and although my hotel was nearby and on dry land, it would have been fun spending the night here in one of the many Art Deco rooms, although as I found out a trip into this bygone era is very expensive.

When launched the Queen Mary was the world's largest ever ship at 75,000 tons, even larger than the Titanic. Plying the North Atlantic route for over 30 years carrying all classes of passengers to the new world from the old world. It also holds the world record for the most number of people on one ship at one time being 16,500 GI soldiers, whilst it was being used as a troop transporter in World War 2. Beside the Queen Mary is a large dome that was built as a museum for the re-built Howard Hughes gigantic Spruce Goose aeroplane, after that the domes use was changed to be the Long Beach cruise ship terminal. Often large cruise ships come alongside their vintage cousin on route to Caribbean destinations. Also,

Long Beach is used as one of the circuits for the Indy Cart Series road racing and in fact it was held here last weekend.

It was a momentous occasion for me as I have never seen the Pacific Ocean, I had seen the Atlantic and the Indian oceans but this was the big one, looking out ahead of me, over the water and you will not hit land until Antarctica, looking to the left being west the next landfall was Papua New Guinea, it was a truly vast ocean.

As the port was not a place to cycle I returned across the bridge to re-trace my steps up the Los Angeles River turning left over the road bridge through Wilmington. It was hell incarnate, trucks and cars whizzing past me with only inches to spare, six lanes of traffic all bullying and vying for space that did not exist, the weakest had no right to be there and in this case, it was me, clearly the honeymoon period of safe cycling was clearly over. I had enough at one point and found a small raised sidewalk and cycled along that running alongside an elevated road and junction with a wire fence beside me.

It felt like a physiological, physical and emotional test, a hunger games for environmental transport. If I survived today I wanted a medal or a T shirt or something-perhaps even a stiff drink later.

Eventually I left the traffic frenzy and found myself in a quiet park next to a large tranquil pond, such bliss. Time to get the heart beat down to below 130 for the first time in an hour and have a chocolate bar. The area that I was travelling in now was decidedly wealthy in comparison to some of the areas I had been through today, I kept following the GPS and it brought me to the door of the

Americas Best value Inn. I had a long chat with the welcoming chap in reception who was fascinated in my journey so far. The room was great and just around the corner from a pizza restaurant which was my meal for tonight. I was pleased that I had made it through the roads today and I will always remember them as the most difficult and most dangerous I have ever cycled in my life and I have cycled in a lot of cities over the last 35 years.

I never had that drink, couldn't even finish my small pizza as I was just too tired and I collapsed once again on the bed and that was that.

The morning in LA was great, it was bright crisp and warm and I was eager to keep exploring, especially the beach up to Santa Monica. Hence, after handing the room key in, I was again on the LA roads but I was no longer a novice, I hit those roads with attitude and determination. I was strongminded that I would be in control of my own space, although the roads did bite back every so often.

One driver sliced past me, so I shouted back "Oi" loudly, as is my prerogative and when I caught up with this reckless driver at the lights I politely said "that was a wee bit close back there mate" and the response which was classic was "I am late for work and you held me up buddy". I can think of many responses now but at the time I was dumfounded that a driver would rather run over a cyclist than be late for work, was this the American ambition for making money overruling basic human nature? You could taste the competitiveness in the air, everyone rushing to fill space on the roads that were clearly already full. Put into that mix a bicycle that moves without hindrance along gridlocked roads and it creates jealously and conflict, why drivers don't just ditch the car and get on a bicycle to join the free movement I will never know.

Only a few more miles of this then I get onto Redondo Beach and I can relax. I endured the last few miles of this crazy traffic and then I was on the cycle path with the beach on my left and exclusive beach house properties on my right, interspaced with small tent cities that formed in spare spaces in-between.

This path will take me north to Santa Monica mainly off road for 15 miles, what bliss. Coming towards me with a clearly heavily laden bike was a happy chap, as I found out was called Brandon and he has essentially been living on and off his bike for a few years and has travelled excessively in North America.

He was making his way south to San Diego to meet up with some of his family. I asked him how he funds his travels and it turns out he is a geologist and sells crystals and rocks, he showed me a collection of some and they were very impressive and he extracts them from the lumps of rock samples he carries, in the evening when wild camping. Now for a cycle tourist weight is an important issue and I can think of better items to carry apart from heavy rocks but that's his trade and it allows him to continue his travels so good luck.

We had a long chat as brothers-on-bikes and he had such an optimistic outlook in life, in fact a very non-confrontational attitude, although he did not know where he was camping every night, that decision was made as and when he felt like stopping. I was jealous of his laissez-faire attitude as I personally need to know minute by minute where I am going and where I am staying even to the point that a reserve plan B is always available if plan A falters.

We said our farewells after exchanging emails and I continue to wish him well in his travels. I have since learnt he works in a bike shop in San Diego. The beach houses on the right were all different, I never saw two that were the same; there was futuristic looking builds, historic looking designs and many varieties in-between. What they all had in common was the splendid views out to sea complete with noisy aircraft constantly landing and taking off at LAX.

The Los Angeles airport was nearly beside me with its double runways which look weird when you first see two aeroplanes taking off or landing side by side over the beach and soaring above the Pacific, before turning towards their final destinations. The path had an assortment of transport techniques from cyclists, skateboarders, electric long boarders, electric scooters and fast pushchairs with a runner pushing behind them, all enjoying the sunshine which only happens around 300 days a year here, compared to around 70 days a year for Cornwall, no contest then.

The beach had golden sands as far as the eye could see and was littered with beach volleyball nets ready for players to use and every couple of hundred yards or so a blue wooden lifeguard station standing on stilts was keeping watch and near the shore the occasional palm tree swayed in the breeze for shade. Then the planes got louder and the beach houses disappeared, clearly I was directly underneath the plane's flight path which was proven when a large wide-body Boeing 777 took off over me and I could clearly see some of its passengers looking out their windows at me, aside from it at the same time was a Southwest Airlines Boeing 737 taking off from the parallel runway.

My journey northwards continued leaving the planes far behind, the next piece of beach is the famous Venice beach with an assortment of shops and cafes alongside, the route ahead was blocked by big burly security guards and some policeman. The reason is that filming was taking place, so we had to wait for the director to shout "cut" before we could continue.

All the film paraphernalia was there, such as a camera on a gimbal, reflect sun screens and support trucks. I did not recognise any of the actors who were being filmed whilst all looking hopelessly into a pram.

Almost immediately there was a sweet smell in the air, I was sure it was cannabis and sure enough over to the side there was a marijuana shop with smokers outside, I assume trying the products, this concept I still find unusual but it is legal to use here in California. I just wonder and worry how many of the dodgy drivers on the roads are actually stoned.

The wooden Santa Monica pier came into view just past the 70's influential Muscle Beach with its bronze Adonis gods working out on the torture frames and swings. The pier was heavily laden with a mixture of roller coasters and Ferris wheel; the cycle path initially took me under the pier and I could look up from the dark tunnel through the gaps in the boardwalk above. I returned back under the tunnel as there was no ramp access to the pier on the north side, once the ramp was found I stopped at the Route 66 sign, indicating that this was the end of the trail and I think as well it is also the start of the 2,448 miles of the "Mother Road" ending in Chicago after travelling through 9 states.

I felt proud as I had traversed some 200 miles on Route 66 on a bicycle. Some motor bikers had clearly covered it all and were being pictured grinning below the sign. I stopped off at Soda Jerks Ice Cream Parlour and had a

Route 66 Special Banana Split which I believe contained everything that could be put into a banana split including marshmallows, strawberry, chocolate, pineapple sauce and vanilla- it was epic.

Back in the UK a chap called Joe had previously emailed me offering to be my host while I was in this area of LA via the *warmshowers* host match website. I was glad as I would be able to spend some time with an American for longer than a brief chat, as I had so many questions for him later about the States.

He lived in Culver City which meant a 10-mile ride back into the throng of downtown LA traffic oh-joy. After the ice cream rush I had plenty of energy to scoot along the livid roads which either had cars moving fast beside me or sat stationary. Not sure which one is better for a cyclist as they both have their implicit dangers to the uninitiated.

The GPS took me straight to the correct address in a residential area just a few blocks south of the main commercial area. Joe welcomed me to his house and helped me to park and lock the bike in his garage around back. Over a Mexican beer we talked about lots of topics and I am sure he must have felt he was being interrogated sometimes but Joe was a font of knowledge.

For food, it was decided to go to a local Greek/Serbian restaurant or was it a Serbian/Greek restaurant? I do not know but I do know that it was not cheap, small beers cost $8 and a speciality salad $14, you get the picture but hey this is LA! The company was as good as the food and I got chatting to the owner on account to my shirt being an Arsenal shirt and his love of football (soccer over here) probably not getting many opportunities to discuss football with many people in America.

He was sorry to see Arsene Wenger retire from running Arsenal and I must say I had to agree with him. Then a woman that Joe knew joined us, she was retired from university teaching I believe and was now a volunteer legal charity worker and we got talking about a very non-American topic- the damage to the environment.

It turns out that the agricultural region of Central Valley has some major environmental concerns with water. This area produces vast amounts of cash crops; in fact 80% of the world's Almonds are grown there for example.

This water intensive agriculture uses both surface water reservoirs and ground water aquifers; sometimes as much as 50% is extracted from underground, depending on the time of year and rainfall and snowfall conditions. These are supplies of water that are thousands of years old and can run out as they are not being re-supplied as fast as being used.

The effect is twofold; farmers need to drill deeper to get to usable water levels which increase extraction costs and as a result the ground level has been sinking in some areas as the water has been extracted. In some places, it can be up to a foot per year that the levels sink. This additional infrastructure repair cost is also expected to grow year on year. She also added that there are some bridges that have sunk so much that they are just above the water level; perhaps I will see some when I cycle through the Central Valley in a few days' time.

After I paid the bill and a tip, it was back to Joe's when Dave another cyclist turned up as he was also staying the night, unusually he did not have a bike yet and was hoping to pick up a cheap one tomorrow morning.

Now that's poor planning, a cycle tour with no bike. After what was a marathon of chatting I said goodnight to Dave and Joe feeling shattered and woozy after a full meal and after only two beers, yep I am turning into a lightweight.

In the morning, I declined coffee as I don't care much for it and packed my panniers and attached them to the bike, after saying cheerio I left Culver City for a short ride north into the Hollywood district. Many thanks to Joe for being a great host in LA.

Ride Data	
Date	1/5/18
Cycling Distance (Miles)	40.36
Cycling Time (Hours)	4:27
Average speed (mph)	9.1
Elevation Gain (feet)	538

Chapter 17

Culver City to Hollywood and other touristy stuff

An unusually short cycle today so I could take it easy and soak up the sights around me. That was the plan but the reality of the ride was once again competitive and hazardous to my health, so full concentration was required to avoid injury or death.

I was passing through some very exclusive neighbourhoods with manicured lawns and trimmed bushy trees with pristine flower beds overflowing in a riot of colours. While others were equipped with security booths and fences and some blocks were clearly gated communities that did not want the riff-raff to get in, with armed security milling about.

Just outside these exclusive neighbourhoods were less affluent areas that felt more open, as residents were walking around and talking to other residents, assisted by the lack of any 20ft high security fences and CCTV cameras.

Then there were seriously deprived neighbourhoods with buildings in poor states of repair, cars and trucks rusting away in driveways and massive ferocious dogs roaming around yards barking warnings to any potential interlopers. The wealth level concentrations were geographical and on streets with no borders to cross, sometimes the quality of the road surface and an increase of potholes reflected the wealth of the neighbourhood that I was in.

Here however, must be bin day as the clearly marked rare cycle path was randomly blocked for about a half-mile with wheelie bins placed within the two lines of the cycle path, weaving in and out of these from path to road and back again was chancy and bothersome and totally preventable with a bit of forethought, proved by some residents who had thoughtfully positioned their bins by the gutter instead.

On the green steep peak, ahead I could see the white HOLLYWOOD sign, this large iconic sign was originally an advertising hoarding for HOLLYWOODLAND housing development that used to be illuminated with bulbs spelling out HOLLY then WOOD and lastly LAND, then in 1949 the LAND and lights were removed to leave the famous sign we see now. In fact, the sign was so dilapidated back in the 1970's benefactors were sought for its refurbishment and one of these was Alice Cooper who paid $28,000 to save the third O.

I cycled into Hollywood and came across Hollywood Boulevard with its throngs of tourists and gift shops and museums, these I would visit tomorrow on my rest day as a safer pedestrian rather than a hot sweaty and dazed touring cyclist.

Once again the GPS took me straight to the Hollywood hotel where unfortunately I was advised during check in that I had to lock the bike outside along an alley running alongside the hotel but it was secure as no-one had access apart from hotel staff and as luck would have it, it was immediately below my hotel room window. As I have a Bluetooth movement alarm *(Sense Peanut)* fitted under the saddle it was within transmitter range of my phone, so any bike movement would sound on my phone as an alarm notifying me of this fact, this helped me to relax.

Every room at the hotel has a movie theme which in reality is just a movie poster in that room, mine was the *Attack of the 50ft women* a 1958 cult sci-fi film. The hotel was a great base both in facilities and location for exploring the attractions and history of Hollywood and its surrounding districts such as Beverly Hills.

After a quick shower, I had a short walk around the corner to meet up with the Access Hollywood Tour that I had previously booked to do the touristy thing and to be driven around in a small tour bus. The purple van with its roof sliced off and replaced with a tarpaulin could sit 10 but today there were 7 of us, being Chris the driver, 3 visitors from Slovakia, 2 Americans and myself, we all sat in the really large comfy seats and were whisked away to start our tour lasting a couple of hours. We were warned to be on our guard as we would frequent the stars and celebrities' favourite places to eat, exercise, shop and also outside some of their homes.

Be ready with the camera as it could just be a brief glimpse of Hugh Grant, Vinnie Jones or hundreds of other supporting actors. Chris did a good job setting the tension to high, as my fellow-hunters were poised ready and feverously scanning the horizon for celebrities of various ilk's. I last felt like this in Kenya whilst doing a safari looking for Elephant, Giraffe or Zebra and spotting them before they disappeared into the bush. Here it had a more urban feel and rather exhausting looking at everyone in the streets who may or may not be an ultra-famous celebrity; if they were around would I spot them?

Probably not, so I left that part of the safari to my colleagues as they seemed much more informed than me. The tour whizzed along streets that housed the rich and famous all behind massive security gates with beefy armed bouncers patrolling around keeping the peasants at bay.

Then we went up to the Hollywood sign and got out of the van to take some pictures and the panorama down the hill looking into LA was breath-taking. It was a clear day with very little pollution so no smog and I could see south to Long Beach where I had cycled up from previously and right below me was the famous Hollywood Bowl open air concert site that has hosted all the well-known performers such as the Beatles, Pink Floyd, Monty Python and The Who.

The trip next went through Beverly Hills with the rich and smart properties surrounding streets full of Tesla's, Ferrari's, Bugatti's and Bentley's. This was the first time I have seen a traffic jam full of cars each worth over £200,000 plus. We went past the Playboy Mansion and Justin Timberlake's humble abode and many, many others who were clearly all out as I failed to see anyone of note just empty exclusive mansions.

We crawled past famous restaurants gawping at their diners who gawped back probably feeling we were intrusive and I must agree it did often feel uncomfortable on this urban human safari. Then a diversion along Rodeo Drive with its flower beds and palm trees along the middle of the road and shops that sell items that are so expensive and exclusive only the mega-rich and royalty could afford to frequent. What I found striking was this was the only shopping street that I did not see any homeless people, litter or pan-handlers about, is there a subliminal message in this? Then back up another steep hill that wound its way up and up to a vantage point that looked north to the massive San Fernando Valley with the Transverse Range of mountains that encircled it in the far distance, a direction I would be cycling in very soon.

We continued along the rim of this hill and could see down to the Griffith Observatory with its three observatory domes, and closer still were a selection of houses that were perched precariously on the side of a steep cliff supported by long thin struts that drove into the rock face below, not somewhere I could live as it is akin to flying i.e. nothing below you.

It was turning colder and Chris being the gent stopped to hand out blankets to any cold passengers who needed them, our tour concluded with a visit along sunset strip to the variety of bars and the iconic Comedy Store and legend full Whisky a Go-Go rock and roll venue. I was now getting cold after hurtling around in an open top van for a few hours, we all said our good-byes and I returned to the hotel to warm up via a subway to scoff a veggie patty.

In the morning breakfast for everyone was in the hotel corridor outside on a shelf, this contained the basic ingredients being cereal, yogurt and fruit juice but no milk, I was advised that I should use hot water with the cereal, no thanks I thought, so I mixed in yogurt with the cereal which made it semi-edible. After this I quickly got some tokens from reception and did a washing load as clean clothes were running dangerously short, whilst waiting for the cycle to cycle, I was able to transfer all the videos and photos to my iPad from yesterday's safari. Once I had fathomed out the intricacies of the dryer and fed it with even more tokens, I had clothes ready to go. Afterwards I checked the map where today's attractions were located and took off on foot.

Today I would visit the Guinness World of Records, Ripley's Believe It or Not and Hollywood Wax Museum which I had pre-booked in the UK at a give-away price. On the way, I passed by Chris waiting in his Access Hollywood van and I asked him for his picture as I had forgotten yesterday. Next thing his boss comes out and offered to take the picture of us both by the mini-bus. Chris is a truly funny and knowledgeable chap who knows his town well and was passionate about sharing it, that's why everyone truly enjoys his trips.

I found the three attractions about a mile up the road, they were interesting and educational places that took ages to walk miles around, it was strange that they were far from busy and in most display rooms I was the only one in there apart from the wax dummies.

The wax museum was better than some I had been to as I could recognise the character without having to resort to looking at the placard to help decipher their identity, even Donald Trump looked a little like Donald Trump. Ripley's was full of unusual facts and stories; he sure was a busy anthropologist who travelled extensively. Guinness was OK but a little limited in its displays, they had gone for a massive display with hands on toys to cater for the younger generation only.

Outside in the street the pan-handlers were everywhere giving out free CD's or Buddhist monk lookalikes giving wristbands to unsuspecting people and then asking for a cash donation of $10. I had already seen a documentary on these rogues and thus real Buddhists monks are getting annoyed at this scam which is growing in all parts of America as it clearly not a positive representation of the Buddhist community.

On the floor beneath me are the stars set in the pavement (sidewalk) being the walk of fame, around 2,500 of them for actors, producers, artists, radio and television, every so often I recognised a name but to walk around its total 1.3 miles looking at the ground seemed exhausting so I gave it a miss, happy that I had seen my two favourite artists being Robin Williams and David Bowie who were just across the road from the well-known legendary Chinese Theatre, the location of many a feature films red-carpeted premiere.

These stars cost the namesake $30,000 to make, set and maintain and will always be located on the sidewalk come what may.

Ride Data	
Date	3/5/18
Cycling Distance (Miles)	12.93
Cycling Time (Hours)	1:40
Average speed (mph)	7.7
Elevation Gain (feet)	520

Chapter 18

Hollywood to Santa Clarita

Yogurt and cereal again for breakfast washed down with fruit juice and I also sneaked a couple of bananas in for later as well. I got the bike out of the alley just in time as the bin men arrived at the same time and they would not have been able to wheel the massive trash bins out past my locked bike, that could have been interesting. The first part of the journey was a massive climb out of Hollywood north into the sprawling San Fernando Valley.

After the big climb up it was a nice ride down into the valley, where the GPS came into its own. As it was threading a quiet route for me through some very large roads and commercial areas and locating some bike paths that I would never have found. In order that I could monitor the upcoming gradient climbs I allowed the GPS to re-calculate today's route which I checked and it seemed fine.

Along the route I encountered many "all way stops", which as a cyclist are far better than their European counterparts being the roundabout. If a junction is controlled as an all-way stop then every access road has a red stop sign, and everyone without exception must stop, if a vehicle gets to a stop line before you then they get to drive off first after first stopping. It allows cyclists to have the same status as any other vehicle thus making for a safer junction, although it is dependent on vehicles stopping in the first place-some don't and drivers need to be observant to maintain the correct order. But it has been proven that these junctions are not as efficient for traffic flow as a roundabout as everyone must stop as opposed to a roundabout where you give way. Some of the roundabouts I have experienced in America have clearly confused everyone so they have put stop signs on their roundabouts in place of yield signs, negating any benefit they would have produced.

The Warner Brothers studio was busy and had some filming taking place as the line of limousines were lining up waiting to go in but alas the black-out windows stopped me identifying any potential Hollywood stars being whisked into work.

Suburb after suburb went past and in one I found it strange that dunes of rubbish lined the street, items such as tables, chairs, wardrobes, cookers, fridges and carpets were piled up on the side of the road. Every house contributed by having their own heap outside their house. The amount of rubbish was staggering, why was this all on the road? Is it some massive clear out after a natural disaster? I decided that after seeing the street cleaning sign posted on the streetlights that there is one day a month that the refuse collectors come and take away house rubbish, in addition to normal garbage and there sure was a massive amount of it. Some piles I calculate equate to my furniture and other household rubbish for about 10 years and this was a month's supply.

Is this how the richest nation stays rich by churning through household goods rapidly? Once again another massive industrial estate became part of my route with massive rigs moving around the narrow streets making for heart in your mouth overtaking moments. I am sure that my rear mirror which I am scanning more and more has avoided a lot of nasty confrontations as it allows me to gauge activity approaching from behind be it threat or friend. The San Fernando Valley was now nearly traversed and the large canyon filled range of mountains was ahead of me, called the Elsmere Canyon Open Space rising 1,500ft above me.

It was now getting hotter with 30 degrees being passed so I pulled over to a store to collect some water before I soon left civilisation once again. The GPS beeped for me to turn right into Silver Oaks Drive which was closed off by a large gate but there was still room for me to squeeze beside a post and the gate. This road under the pylons was clearly abandoned to traffic but was still being used as a path northwards into the canyons ahead.

I dutifully followed the GPS onwards into sparser terrain that became very steep and remote. There was not a soul about, I had the entire valley to myself and the only human interference was from massive pylons that zig-zagged up the peaks ahead of me. Gosh it was getting hotter so taking stock of my water levels, I had 4 litres left, however I always keep 1.5 litres in reserve just in case so I had 2.5 litres remaining- that should be fine I calculated.

I carried on the small dirt trail that continued snaking around the base of the peaks with growing ravines on one side and steep cliffs the other. At one point the path had a large crack all along its middle and it was clear that it had started to landslide into the ravine below, it would fall at some point, not today but after the next heavy rainfall I venture. The steepness of the track increased so

I had to dismount and push from the rear of the bike upwards to stop the front wheel from lifting off the ground and bringing the bike crashing in a pile, sometimes I failed and the bike did smash into the dirt with me cursing and swearing, today was turning into a traumatic and exhausting trudge.

It was now a foot slog with an unwieldly heavy bike with total drag weight of 45kg, I was getting worn-out. This can't go on for much longer I thought, the trail started around 2 miles ago and I must be able to see the top of the peak I was circling around, perhaps around the next corner became the driving influence. Alas, the next corner resulted in a steeper gradient and I was dragging the bike 10ft stopping for a rest for a minute and then another 10ft. This progress was slow; I was drinking more and more water to try and recover from the constant struggle.

Then a disaster, the path ahead of me had previously collapsed into a 20ft wide hole around 10ft deep with no path left around it, I just looked at it in disbelief trying to work out a way forward. I decided that I would carry a piece of luggage at a time around the side of the narrow rim of this crater. It was high and slim but I hoped with smaller amounts of weight I could maintain my balance and get through by stepping stones method on some of the rocks protruding from the crater. I took the rack pack first as it was lightest and being careful where to step I traversed the hole successfully.

After repeating this bouldering tactic many times, I was across, bringing the un-laden bike last which I swung around as a counterbalance.

The onward path turned into just a rough track with nettles and thorns attacking my legs, yet there was no sign of its end. Then fear started to rise in me, doubts about my knowledge of the route, foolishly allowing the GPS to dictate the trail to me, getting into a situation that was now becoming dangerous.

With little water supplies and surrounded by steep sided canyons and no sign of roads or paths I was dicing with a potential disaster. I had to take the decision what to do, I checked the Google Earth on my phone but unknown to me my phone provider had decided to block my account as it was being used in the USA, even though I had already set this up before I left.

I now had limited information available and no communications should something occur, the odds were stacking up against me. I took the disappointing but obvious decision to re-trace my steps back to civilisation. Going back down the hill although a lot easier was depressing as any gains made were now gone.

The result was that I had lost 3 hours on that excursion into the canyon and was completely shattered. I was left with dwindling water and food supplies but thankfully I was out of danger. I blamed the GPS routing that got me in this mess, I am sure it was set on outback horse mode and not bicycle mode, should such a setting exist (which it doesn't), from now on I must fully check the day's route the night before to avoid any repetition of this caper.

After a few miles, back on the safer route I found a small shop and I gulped down two cold diet Cokes one after the other and restocked my water supply, convincing myself to put this learning opportunity behind me.

I joined the Sierra highway through the San Fernando pass and once through the junction a police car and a cop blocked the road. Now this was the only direct road and I had to get through it as there were no suitable replacements for me as a cyclist.

I approached the traffic officer ready to plead my case, he was currently standing by his car busy on the phone, he looked up and saw me approaching and he just waved me onto the closed road. So, the road was empty up to the pass and it turned out that it was mine, all mine, for the next 8 glorious miles. No traffic to worry me, I enjoyed the ride up although I was not sure why traffic was being stopped back at the junction. Then it became apparent as next to an old gas station was all manners of filming trucks, catering, make-up and crew vehicles all parked along the road.

Clearly I had entered a film set, so I tentatively proceeded trying to gauge from people's reaction if I had spoilt all their hard work by cycling into shot of a western movie or some zombie disaster movie, I could not tell and currently there was no-one around to ask. I carried on up the hill and every so often some lights or generators were being packed away by the crew who did not seem to mind me being there, from that I concluded that whatever the filming was about it had now finished. I then topped the hill and had a great long traffic free, white knuckle, streaming eyes, helmet lifting, descent into Santa Clarita- great fun and cooling as well. I met up with a quiet cycle path which ran alongside the Santa

Clara River which was currently fully dried up and judging by the size of the bridges and the width of the watercourse this must be an impressive sight in full flow. Crossing over the I5, I could see the Sky Tower of the Six Flags Magic Mountain theme park close by with the sound of screaming kids piercing through the motorway sounds. A few more corners and then into the motel entrance lane.

Then the repetitive process of checking into another motel started, although I would find out in this one that sleep would be at a premium, due to the constant noises above me all night long.

Ride Data	
Date	5/5/18
Cycling Distance (Miles)	38.96
Cycling Time (Hours)	4:55
Average speed (mph)	7.9
Elevation Gain (feet)	3,288

Chapter 19

Santa Clarita to Palmdale

I would like to say I woke up but alas I hadn't been asleep much, there was just too much noise emanating from the room above, which was either a dodgy movie film set or a honeymoon suite, either way the bed rocking and creaking ensured that I could only sleep whilst wearing noise cancelling earphones, which are at best difficult to sleep in!

I had considered going to reception to complain but I was at a loss what to say to them- what would you say?

During one of the many wee small hours that I found myself awake I checked my route on Google Earth to try and avoid a repetition of the poor guidance and non-existent roads I found myself on yesterday.

I discovered that my planned route north to Gorman to pick up the Interstate 5 to cross the Fort Tejon State Historic Park and its mountain range was seriously flawed. The Google Earth images showed that the I5 did not allow cycles as per the signs on the on-ramps.

There was no other way through apart from a small off-road trail through the forests, which after the previous day's experience would not be suitable for a fully laden bike. I had no choice but to rapidly change my route to head east over to Palmdale and pick up the Mojave Desert to cross that way north-west to Bakersfield. This meant that my planned rest day in Bakersfield was binned, so in a panic I franticly adjusted all the affected bookings on the Internet and now had to look forward to an additional 60 miles and a few exhausting days in the high, hot, windy and dry Mojave Desert.

Time to head out east, to ascend the 2,500ft range of mountains to head towards the Mojave Desert, the road was the Soledad Canyon Road. The climb was quite gentle on an old road that was clearly once the main road at some point in the past, due to the size of the bridges and tunnels that it went over and through.

Once again I ran alongside the railway line which was running in the canyon far below me and our paths criss-crossed throughout the day. The Santa Clara dry riverbed was also a constant companion as we followed it upriver to the source in the mountains.

It became dry, hot and the bushy trees started to disappear being replaced with shrubs in the rocks beside the road. This was turning into rattle snake country and this was confirmed when I saw a few flat ones on the roadside.

As I was approaching one of the long dark tunnels cut through the rocky canyon sides, I waited outside as I could see that there was no shoulder inside the dark and gloomy passageway. I looked back and listened to make sure that I could not see or hear any traffic coming up behind, it was clear and quiet so I dashed into the tunnel hoping that I would not have to share it with any vehicles whilst inside its clutches. Fortunately, I managed to get through before anyone else- what a victory. I was now about half way up the side of the cliff looking down to the dry river bed and the railway line elevated above it, when a double-decker commuter train racing towards Los Angeles sped past. I read that in a decade, this canyon will be home to the new California high speed rail project. Potentially travelling up to 220mph and reducing the journey time from LA to San Francisco to two and a half hours for a 400-mile journey. California is still an environmental beacon for the rest of the States, contrary to the current political theatre and one of the main driving force is the 40% less emissions expected by passengers taking an electrified train in place of fossil fuelled cars or planes.

The hill was finally broken at an altitude of 3,000ft and it felt swelteringly hot, the route took me over the California Aqueduct, a 400-mile-long man-made snaking river that collects water from Northern California and distributes to water thirsty agriculture and cities further south.

Back in the 1980's, cyclists could follow the oh-so flat smooth tarmac beside the canal around California, alas that was stopped in 1988. All around me was a massive flat plateau surrounded by mountains in the far distance with a shimmering fuzzy heat haze blocking out the finer details. I crossed over the subterranean San Andres fault 10 miles below me, relocating from the Pacific tectonic plate to the North American tectonic plate without a murmur or even a shudder. These plates are aggressively moving against each other by 1 to 1.5 inches a year but today they seem happy with each other.

I also read that the incidence of a major earthquake is in the region of once every 140-160 years and its currently about 60 years overdue. I put that thought to the back of the mind, as there is clearly nothing I can do about it either now or over the next 2 weeks when I will be criss-crossing this fault and others on my non-earthquake proof, fully susceptible bicycle. I was now in the high desert and I could feel the increasing heat as beads of sweat started to run down my face, this would be the norm for the next few days and I promised myself that at any available store or gas station I would stop, drink a litre and buy sufficient water to replace any used, so that I could maintain my fluids.

The city of Palmdale was large with a population of over half a million inhabitants and was very spread out with major roads running through its middle. These I negotiated whilst starting to trust the GPS, I had to have full confidence in it once the again, as although I had the paper maps, their scales were painfully large. I eventually made it to the north of the city and found my motel, although it was in a very industrial part of Palmdale it did have a Taco Bell nearby which meant that dinner was totally sorted.

Ride Data	
Date	6/5/18
Cycling Distance (Miles)	41.09
Cycling Time (Hours)	5:22
Average speed (mph)	7.7
Elevation Gain (feet)	3,494

Chapter 20

Palmdale to Mojave

I achieved a bit more sleep last night than previously which is good for morale, also the room was equipped with a fridge so I chilled all my water, hoping it should stay cooler for a bit longer during the day.

Breakfast was not bad but consisted of the same cereal with milk and copious amounts of fruit juice. The scrambled egg looked beaten up and old so I gave it a miss, a dodgy stomach on a bike is not a good idea.

This morning I will make a slight detour to visit the Blackbird museum, as after all this is the home of the Skunk Works assembly building, which is part of the Lockheed Martin Aerospace Corporation.

This part of Palmdale has a superb off road cycle path which is wide and well maintained running beside the road network but unsurprisingly no one is using it, this could be due to the heat or just that that distances to anywhere here are just so vast, so it's probably a weekend warriors bike route. After half an hour in the early morning growing heat the shape of a variety of planes appeared beside the road with the Blackbird's in prime position.

The Lockheed SR-71 Blackbird was a reconnaissance plane capable of exceeding Mach 3 and during the height of the cold war was often spying above war zones and probably the USSR as well. This plane was essentially impossible to shoot down as it flew higher than any enemy attack plane and faster than any of the surface to air missiles aimed at it. In fact, if the pilot detected a radar missile lock all they did was put their foot down and scoot away, as proven during the Vietnam War, when over 800 missiles were fired at the Blackbird and not one found its target. The plane was also unique at the time for its titanium metal construction for strength and heat tolerances.

The large amount of titanium required for their build was not available in the USA. So, the Skunk Works had to purchase massive amounts of titanium ore via intermediator countries and they had to create bogus companies, as the only main source was from the USSR, which is rather ironic. In all 32 of these SR-71's Blackbirds were built at the nearby Skunk Works and with impressive statistics, such as 2,200mph cruising speed and 80,000ft operating maximum ceiling they did set their place in the history books, before retiring in 1998.

Looking at the two here at the museum they still look imposing and menacing and were literally pushing the envelope of available technology when first flown in 1966. Considering 12 planes were lost due to mechanical issues over its life-span it is a testament of the brave pilots to even set foot in one of these rocket chariots.

The other plane of note here at the museum was the specially adapted Boeing 747 that I had watched on TV as a kid back in 1977 transporting one of the space shuttles, it was lumbering ungainly with the heavy 75-ton spaceship being given a piggy-back on its top fuselage.

Now to re-trace my path back up the road to head north out of Palmdale which took me past the Skunk Work Lockheed Martin building with the famous black and white skunk logo on its side. This is the site that is building the Royal Navy's new F-35 Lightning II multirole aircraft for the Queen Elizabeth Class aircraft carriers which we will be seeing lots of over the next 50 years.

I kept peddling as the security around here was obviously rather tight and before I knew it I was back in the empty desert with another railway line beside me and flanked by mountains around the perimeter of my vision, with a few stray mountains individually popping up many thousands of feet high to help break up the vast plateaus flatness.

I was now back in the full swing of desert life on a bike, staying cool by pouring water over my sun scarf and maintaining a comfortable speed without too much exertion, a balancing act of speed versus energy use, versus the subsequent body heat that it produced.

Joshua trees with limbs outstretched guided me northwards as they had done for the 19th century Mormon settlers previously; they had named them Joshua, after the biblical figure. On the ground the vegetation of the Brittle Bush, Common Saltbush and Creosote Bush gave green tints to the otherwise brown landscape and slithering in-between could be found the Glossy Snake, Mojave Rattlesnake and the Gopher snake, of which I only saw flattened versions, fortunately for me.

Every so often small dust spirals would appear in the distance and these small *Dust Devils* although short lived were fascinating to watch for their ghost-like unruly spiral dance which soon died away leaving just a few marks in the sand where they once reigned. This being a minor road the traffic was thankfully very light, however, an occasional vehicle did go past me a lot slower than the rest, I think this was to make sure that I was OK, as after all the desert is a place that everyone looks out for each other, mistakes here in 35-degree bone dry heat can be costly, so I appreciated the watchfulness being shown by my fellow-humans as a refreshing change to nearly being run over by them.

One car did fully stop and the driver lowered the window and after grimacing with the heat that hit his face he said "are you lost bud?", I explained that all was going swimmingly and I was great, "are you Australian?", this was becoming the stock response, so after politely correcting him on my nationality he checked that I had enough water and that I knew what I was doing and that I possessed all my faculties, he wished me luck before closing his window and returning to his air-conditioned cocoon and driving off with a trail of desert dust following in his wake.

Thanks to the heat and the ultra-low humidity, I started to suffer again with some nosebleeds, which after a while did stop, just an occupational hazard in the dry atmosphere, just need to remember to stay hydrated. The rest of the body was faring well and by not using the pedal cleats all day long and resorting to the flat pedal side I had avoided a major pain I used to get in my right foot. I just used the cleats for tough hills to provide upstroke power and for bumpy descents when I needed my feet secured in place.

I was pleased about this discovery, as I was worried before the trip that this agonising foot pain would return due to the high mileage and pedalling time. I had found its cause successfully, even though it had taken me nearly 10 years of experimenting with a variety of approaches. The one part of my body that was hurting religiously after three hours cycling each day was my right shoulder. This was previously operated on due to an *impingement syndrome* back in 2001 and I assume makes this area more susceptible to wear and tear. So, when it got bad it was time to hop off the bike and swing my arms about and by doing a standing rear arch manoeuvre with elbows back, it did help ease some of the pain, I must have looked like a right berk beside the road doing yoga poses but it was necessary to keep the pain in check and being tolerable.

The main highway 14 went straight through the middle of Mojave town, slicing across and separating the town with one side for the train tracks and the other side for the hotels, businesses and fast food outlets.

It was loud, noisy, dusty and smelt sooty from the tail-end exhausts of the thousands of vehicles that passed through its middle. I took refuge along a side street to avoid the six-lane motorway and before I knew it I was outside the Motel 6.

At reception, the receptionist could not find my booking, which was a surprise, I felt a little worried but given the number of motels around me I am sure I could get another room somewhere. Then he eventually said "is it this Motel 6 or the other Motel 6 up the road that you want?" Why did he not say that earlier, it transpired that there were two Motel 6 establishments within half a mile of each other. I said cheerio and joined the frantic highway 14 for a brief ride north up to the other Motel 6 which was thankfully on a much quieter part of town, further away from the constant rumblings of the road and hooting of the trains. After checking into the room in a lodge like complex I did some laundry in the washing-machine whilst drinking vast quantities of ice cold diet coke from the soda machine beside it.

The crystal-clear swimming pool out front looked so inviting in this blistering heat but so far I had avoided any major sun-burn and wished to keep it that way so I kept vampire wary of the strong sun.

A stroll down to *Subway* for tonight's small meal allowed me to see the various eating houses alongside the road but so far I had not seen any pub equivalents here in the States, all the ones I had seen did beer with your food-I just wanted a beer on its own. I think they call these "dive bars" in America and I had not yet seen one, well one that looked welcoming anyway.

The subway technician was very chatty and she was amazed at my trip so far and was very interested in the differences I had seen between the UK and USA. I said that there were both many and none depending on your bank-balance viewpoint.

But more importantly the American subways were far superior as they offered sliced Avocado as an extra to their sandwiches, result.

Ride Data	
Date	7/5/18
Cycling Distance (Miles)	44.34
Cycling Time (Hours)	4:33
Average speed (mph)	9.7
Elevation Gain (feet)	572

Chapter 21

Mojave to Bakersfield

Overnight it was quite the riot when a couple of families that were staying in the lodge building opposite had a blazing row around midnight that turned loud and aggressive.

I was expecting the cops to turn up, guns ablaze, smashing down doors and throwing people on car hoods, well that's only in the movies, the reality was that it all calmed down as quickly as it started and the still quiet air returned. I still had my bike behind the door as an additional barrier of defence as if that would make any difference to a crazed madman brandishing a Magnum 45.

Breakfast was consistently sparse but I managed to squirrel away some food both by eating it and hoarding some away for later, as today I needed plenty of calories. It was going to be the longest mileage day of the trip so far, at 70 miles plus and 4,000ft elevation gain in the desert heat reaching 34 degrees plus.

I hit the road at 6am due to it being slightly cooler and the wind was less powerful at that time. It was straight out of the motel and onto the desert within minutes, looking behind after I got some elevation I saw hundreds of older commercial aircraft neatly lined up on the side of the Mojave Air and Space Port, some clearly awaiting dismantling and disposal, while others are there for long term mothballed storage for airlines.

Mojave is chosen given its low humidity, little rainfall and therefore minimal corrosion which benefits the components and airframe. It was an impressive site seeing these old wide body aircraft such as DC-10's, Tri-Star's and Boeing 747's glinting in the morning sun with a majestic orange glow surrounding them.

The strange light also made the massive wind farm around me seem surreal with its hundreds of turbines turning in response to the wind coming up from the valley ahead of me.

A turning wind turbine means wind and unfortunately for me I was heading north west which is straight into the prevailing wind that was feeding these turbines. The terrain was due to peak at 4,840ft after the first 13 miles, after that the rest of today's run should be mostly downhill, I hoped. The wind was getting stronger the higher up I climbed and it was now around 15mph, even at 8am in the morning, this did concern me as a headwind was now likely most days until I reached San Francisco, as my direction was heading into the prevailing wind.

I do however have a very unusual view of headwinds, ask most cyclist and it's the worst thing ever but I have cycled John O'Groats to Lands' End twice which is opposite to most people's choice of direction. This resulted in a headwind every day for which although annoying did cool me down. I have done other long distance rides which had a tail wind and I found myself overheating and sweating profusely. This is something that does not happen when you have a strong headwind, so one small silver lining to an otherwise dark cloud. Either way, I had no control of it and I had to cycle in this direction so just accept it, or that's what I told myself anyway. The road eventually started its slow decent and the terrain and vegetation around me was also slowly changing, smoother mountains appeared and they had more sporadic green bushes growing on them. I crossed behind Tehachapi town and could see the wide Freeway 58 emerging from the mountain and weaving its way north-west to the pass ahead.

My road was a riot of switch-back corners all downhill for many miles, cars had to queue behind me as although they were faster than me along the brief straights they were slower than me around the many convoluted hairpins, so we all mutually stayed in this line going downhill, it was great to see a car happily sit behind me whilst protecting my rear.

Every so often I pulled over to let them pass only to catch up with them shortly afterwards on the twisty corners. This was great exhilarating fun which was only slightly spoilt by the unprotected massive drops down the roadside to a certain ugly demise should I over cook any of the corners, so concentration was high and focused. Eventually the twists came to an end and I was faced with a junction and a choice, left to the highway 58 and straight on to continue my route, according to the GPS.

I also saw the sign on the on ramp of the 58 which indicated cycles were prohibited so I would obviously remain on the GPS route.

I carried on and the road got narrower and the tarmac ceased leaving a dirt road but I continued undiminished onwards. The road became a path and then a narrow trail and then a gravel track. It went up then down and followed the railway line very closely; in fact it became too lumpy to cycle safely so I resorted to pushing the bike in an alarming repetition of a few days ago outside Los Angeles.

I continued hoping for the road to break through at any time, if I retraced my steps this time I would have to return up the twisty road all uphill for about 5 miles so with this in mind I soldiered on.

I once again checked Google Earth for any additional guidance and low and behold I found out that the phone company had blocked me once again, even after sorting it out yesterday, wow great timing Yoda-phone, are you trying to kill me? A few freight trains went by slowly with the train crew looking at me pushing a bike essentially along the side of the tracks with no visible path, "look there goes another nutter on a bike" they were probably thinking.

To my left was a ranch with signs showing trespassers will be dealt with harshly and behind that further back over the hill I could hear the busy highway 58. The GPS beeped advising me to turn left but there was a high wire fence to my left and anyway there was no discernible path unless you count a rabbit run. This was getting just far too silly; it was getting overly hot once again and I was not keen on going through the GPS trail challenge twice.

The last straw was a disused bridge where the GPS said I should go next but it was blocked with keep out, danger of collapse, all on large signs that clearly meant business.

I sat down considering my options, I could continue onwards not knowing how long this would go on for as my map data was limited or change tact completely. I decided to go back a short distance to the ranch where I could hear highway 58 to see if I could somehow access that road. Although it was illegal to cycle on I would at least be moving in the right direction and away from this completely remote area in the mountains. So back along the railway line waving at the freight train crews going past who initially hesitated to wave back as they were not used to seeing people around these remote parts.

Then the first ranch that I came across was on my right, with the too high to climb fence but I could hear the busy freeway tantalisingly close, about a quarter of a mile behind the field of long grass and trees.

I would prefer to find somewhere to lift the bike over with its luggage all attached over any fence or gate, as it would be quicker to scarper if caught.

Then a stroke of luck as I spied a gate which was only tied shut with rope and after untying it, I wheeled the bike through into the long grass making sure to re-attach the rope afterwards.

I legged it through that field as I was starting to imagine cowboys riding up and lassoing me whilst shooting guns into the air, or being taken out by a lone sniper security guard. Looking at the grass intently trying to spot imaginary bear traps or anything else the mind can conquer up during times of panic.

The road was getting louder so I was going in the right direction but this was a motorway how was I going to access it successfully and how long before the cops pulled me over, albeit very slowly. Ahead I could see another gate however this one was locked; it was leading up to a path near the concrete wall at the side of the freeway. So, close I had to clear this last gate and enter the state highway land where I could still be arrested but unlikely shot as a trespasser. The gate was on a steep incline and I considered that if I put the bike on its side I could drag it under the small gap from the dirt to the bottom of the gate.

After tipping the bike over on the non-chain side I went over the fence first and lent through and dragged and pulled the bike with the front wheel, it was the closest of margins but after stepping on the pannier to make it thinner it started to inch through. After a few minutes of tugging and pulling it was through the shut gate, I was now just a stone's throw from the road, getting ready for my next felonious action.

Checking the bike over and re-aligning the handlebars to the direction of the front wheel as they had become twisted in the struggle, it was good to go and by quickly lifting the bike with luggage on over the 3ft concrete barrier I found myself on the highway shoulder, trying to be invisible and nonchalant as I could. Fortunately, the freeway was on the hill going down, so before I know it I was up to around 30mph, I just had to make it to the next junction before being spotted by the Highway Patrol. Ten minutes later I took the junction and re-set the GPS to get me away from the freeway and started heading towards Bakersfield.

It beeped as it had made the connections, so I proceeded to follow it once more encouraged now by the size of the road I was on and I was confident in its ability for it to stay a road for the next few miles.

I did stop and had a chat with a workman having his lunch in his car who was not sure how long the road went on for but agreed with me that apart from the freeway there must be another way through the valley.

I continued happily believing that I had put the worst behind me and that I would not end up being deported from America for trespassing or riding illegally on a motorway. This conviction continued for the next 5 miles when I saw a chap cutting his grass on a large sit on mower, I pulled over and after signalling to him that I would like a chat he stopped the engine and said "what's up?", I asked him if this road joined up with the road to Bakersfield further up and he replied "this is the main road that was used before they built the freeway but since then it has been built over and stops just around the hill over there".

I felt like crying and I explained what had happened to get me onto this road and he was surprised as he had sometimes seen cyclists on the freeway but was unaware that it was prohibited traffic. Then his neighbour drove past and pulled over due to the commotion of a bicycle and a grass cutter stopped on the side of the road, he was apprised of the situation by his mate who started with "This Australian cyclist is trying to get through to Bakersfield…." I did not have the energy to correct him this time and his mate said that it was daft that cycles were not allowed on the only road through.

We all agreed that I should make a run for it on the freeway and if caught plead my sorry case. I thanked my fellow felons for their help and they wished me good luck. I once again retraced my long route back to the freeway junction and I started to cycle on the on-ramp heading towards the direction of Bakersfield. Then I saw it, the prohibited traffic sign that read as follows; "Pedestrians" *new-line* "Motor driven" *new-line* "cycles" *new-line* "prohibited", I was a full-sized, grown-up, peanut brained buffoon! The bit I assume where bicycles could be entered was clearly blanked out. America called cycle's bicycles, when I had seen cycles on the sign I had failed to realise that they meant "Motor driven cycles", whatever they were.

I was fully within my rights to use this road as I was on a bicycle and that was not included on the sign. I felt a mixture of complete relief and even greater stupidity for allowing myself to not only add an additional 60-mile day cycling to my plan but also to expose myself to being arrested for trespassing with a bike whilst crossing a ranch, here far out in the wild-west.

I continued sheepishly on the freeway for around 10 more miles and left at the junction joining the much quieter Bena Road which descended through massive canyons on each side; this was clearly the old road as it was wide, well maintained and with big bridges but with very little traffic.

The long sweeping corners were a joy to ride on as there was virtually no traffic, so I could take any line that I wanted to maximise the speed for the exit and in next to no time the mountains were behind me. Spread out in front of me was the massive central valley, the agricultural powerhouse of California and once again the railway line my constant companion came alongside me once again. The city of Bakersfield was getting closer ahead so the roads grew busier and space was more at a premium requiring the senses to attune to the traffic movements, being both defensive and responsive to real time threats, the constant buzz of cycling in a new city is always exiting.

I was glad at the end of the ride as today had been a real challenge both mentally and physically and I needed some rest, so after another *Subway* it was a few minutes watching the *Maze Runner* on TV and then I drifted off.

Ride Data	
Date	8/5/18
Cycling Distance (Miles)	70.73
Cycling Time (Hours)	7:59
Average speed (mph)	8.9
Elevation Gain (feet)	3,925

Chapter 22

Bakersfield to Lost Hills

"I think I broke it!" I said to my fellow-guests in the breakfast room, I was trying to make a pancake using the complex oyster clam grill by following the brief instructions stencilled to its lid.

Instructions: pour pancake mix available from dispenser into griddle after first twisting pan 180 degrees, then seal shut and rotate around another 180 degrees whilst setting timer. It seemed simple enough but perhaps I overfilled it, after seeking assistance from someone, it appeared that the previous user had turned it off, so it was too cold. 20 minutes later I had on my plate a lump of hot yellowish gunge that tasted like the paper plate it was on, after drowning it in maple syrup it turned from a bland taste into a very sickly-sweet bland damp paper plate taste. Last seen being dumped in the trash!

I decided to stick with cereal in future I could handle the complexities of cereal and milk far better.

I was ready to leave and after packing the bike I rolled it through the tight corridors to the lift door. After squeezing the bike into the cramped lift by holding up the front wheel, I selected the first floor (remember: ground floor in the UK) after promising to send it back up for the other fuming guests who could not get in because of me filling it up.

The bottom floor lift door went straight out into the car park and when the lift door opened unfortunately both the bike and me fell out and landed ungainly on the tarmac in a messy pile. After checking the bike was not damaged and everything was pointing the correct way I pushed off west out of Bakersfield city which meant following the Kern River on a purpose made cycle path. The Yokuts Park beside me was alive with movement and after checking closer it was due to hundreds of potentially bubonic-plague carrying squirrels, bouncing around having some serious fun. They had appeared to take over the park and the resultant pot marked ground resembling the craters of the moon.

I had read that one desperate method employed to remove them from an affected area was to pump in propane and oxygen and then set a spark.

The resultant explosion would collapse the deep tunnels and the confined concussion shock kills the little blighters, not sure about the ones near the surface, I assume that they get blown out like a cannonball and become flying squirrels? Either way they were fun to watch in the park frolicking about as if they owned it, I half expected to see some on the swings and a couple on the see-saw entertaining themselves.

Eventually Bakersfield city ended and I found myself in the crop fields but not just any crop fields, these were town sized fields growing a variety of crops, such as; grapes, almonds, strawberries, oranges, walnuts, apricots, dates, figs, kiwi fruit, nectarines, olives, pistachios, prunes, walnuts, lemons, avocados, melons, peaches and plums, these are all grown in California during the year. The area I was in was mainly growing almonds and pistachio nuts and these massive super plantations spread out into the far distance. These would be my new companions for most of the day on both sides of the road and every so often a group of farmers would wave and say "Hola" as I passed by, I would say good morning and wave back to which they would return to their tasks on the trees they were pruning etc.

In the town of Shafter, I called into a drug store for some pain killers as my shoulder was getting worse every day and whilst at the checkout I was asked for ID, "what for?" I asked, "To check you are over 21" she said, "wow, how old do you think I am?" I replied. I did tell her that she was the first person in about 30 years that had asked me to confirm I was old enough, so I felt a growing smugness. In the absence of an American driving licence I handed over my British passport but she could not find my date of birth part. I pointed out the date of birth entry on the page and she replied "That's fine; I can see here that you are 65 years old", "No! That says I was born in 1965, I am 53 not 65" I said, feeling my ego deflate rapidly.

Anyway, the transaction was completed and after paying about five times as much for painkillers than in the UK I bid her a good afternoon.

Then into the Dollar Store for some trail mix and some water and at the checkout I was speaking to a young chap on the till who was planning to cross the States on a bike in a couple of years' time. He was worried about the accommodation cost so I advised him of the cyclist's host scheme at *Warmshowers.org*. It was if he had been handed the missing piece of a 50,000-piece jigsaw, he was over the moon and I reckon when he got home he would be busy planning his trans-USA trip.

Shafter was a nice typical small town America, with cars parked at an angle on each side of Main Street which is great for plenty of parking spaces but not so good for cyclists as cars are reversing out of spaces essentially completely blind, quite a few times in America these reversing cars forced me to swerve or brake hard but for once I felt for the drivers as you just can't see.

Then after leaving the town of Wasco I had a sinking feeling in the rear, my first puncture of the trip. Given the amount of steel wire imbedded in the shreds of truck tyres on the shoulders, I was surprised it took this long to get a puncture, so I took it in my stride and anyway it was in the mid 30's, not the temperature to get worked up into a lather.

There was no shade anywhere, I would have to fix it in the direct sunlight, and so I stripped the bike of its luggage and myself of my helmet, gloves and Hi-Viz and put on the disposable gloves as this needed grubby chain handling.

I have fixed many punctures over the years so was very much in autopilot mode, undo rear calliper brake cable, cover saddle, turn bike upside down, remove pinhead locking axle with key, take off chain from cassette and remove wheel. Then remove one side of tyre and extract inner tube, pump up and at the same time, listen, look and feel on the face for a hole.

I quickly found a small hole and repaired it with a patch, however a word of advice, which I have learnt the hard way previously, make sure you visually check both the inside and outside of the tyre, pulling out any remaining shards or else you will just get another puncture a mile down the road. I pulled out a razor sharp ultra-thin piece of wire using pliers and quickly ran my finger around the inside feeling for any left-over sharps. Then re-assemble trying not to use tyre levers as these should only be used to take the tyre off, use a toe clip strap to hold the tyre in place and use your hands and fingers to replace the tyre on the rim, the last tight bit of tyre I usually use my foot to slide it back on.

Remember: using a tyre lever to put a tyre back on will result in a new puncture in most cases so avoid if possible, please let me share that nugget of information, which I wish someone had told me after fixing puncture after puncture whilst in the wilds of windy and rainy Highlands of Scotland.

Now back on the road I noticed that higher gears on the front chaining were not available so after pulling over I saw that the gear cable was badly frayed near the front derailleur clamp.

This I decided could wait until tonight to replace in the motel room, I had enough gears for the rest of today, I just had to increase my cadence up a bit, that's all. The bike had so far travelled 800 plus miles on this trip over a variety of surfaces with absolutely no ill-effects but now I had my first puncture and the gear cable was ready to snap, what I wonder will be the third problem in the usual trio? It was nice to be moving again as it gave me an opportunity to cool down after sitting in the heat for so long and apart from the gear selection the bike was responding well. Today's motel was just before Lost Hills in a service area for the nearby Interstate 5 which was just a few miles ahead. However, as seems to be the case for me everything does not happen easily, the tell-tale road work signs with the two red diagonal flags appeared and beyond that a massive dust cloud with gravel and tarmac trucks disappearing into it ahead, it was a colossal road works site. Me and my little bike had to find a way through on the bridge going over the I5 to get to the motel the other side but the shoulder had gone and there was a constant flow of trucks trundling each and every way across. I couldn't walk across as there was no sidewalk so I would have to fight it out with the traffic but a steep slope up to the bridge would keep my speed low which is not a good idea. Additionally, access to the bridge was regulated by a contra-flow controlled by workman with stop/go paddles at each end, seeing that gave me an idea.

I approached the bridge cycling on the extreme right hand side of the road to avoid the close passing trucks and taking a deep breath and checking the rear was clear I entered the massive dust cloud, tanking it as fast as I could to get to the start of the contra-flow.

I managed to get there before any trucks and the florescent jacket workman saw me approaching through the dust and immediately understood my plight. He radioed through to his colleague at the other end and they stopped all the traffic crossing the bridge and proceeded to let me through, marvellous I had the bridge to myself, I thanked both workers when I passed them by and I think by their reaction they were glad to help and stop the dust being stirred up around them for at least a few minutes.

I had cleared the bridge roadworks and ahead was the service area with motels and every restaurant you could think of, there was *Mc Donald's, Burger King, Taco Bell, Subway, Jack in the Box, Wendy's* and *Pizza Hut*, I was spoilt for choice for tonight's meal. Before that I replaced the worn-out gear cable with a nice new shiny one, noting that the old one was about one thread away from snapping, also I checked the spokes were still evenly taught since all the bumpy surfaces that had been ridden on over the last few weeks could have created havoc with them.

Ride Data	
Date	9/5/18
Cycling Distance (Miles)	49.77
Cycling Time (Hours)	4:59
Average speed (mph)	10
Elevation Gain (feet)	36

Chapter 23

Lost Hills to Coalinga

A nice early start once again and I was pleased that the gear change was now fully functioning and slick. Today's route will have me brushing alongside the mountain range to the left of the central valley in preparation to crossing over it tomorrow.

I think that this is the best route to San Francisco as the mountains should become a natural barrier to the prevailing wind, the alternative and more popular route of the Pacific highway 1 would have me facing an unchecked strong headwind straight off the ocean every day.

Just outside of the town of Lost Hills there was a very strong pungent smell which became fiercer the closer I got to an odd-looking scrapyard in the distance. The scrapyard appeared to be moving as I got closer, then I could see that there were lots of separate parts stirring and the associated smell was becoming overpowering. I then entered the most bizarre man-made environment, being hundreds upon hundreds of groaning, gyrating and hypnotic pumps, commonly known as nodding donkeys. They were all shapes and sizes; some were hissing and others sloshing, busy in their constant singular task of raising smelly crude oil from the bowels of the Earth and pumping it to a central storage tank.

All around me the machines were in control of my views, they produced the smells and they orchestrated the sounds, there was no life here be it any large vegetation or any flying bird, it was devoid of naturalness. I stopped to take some pictures and almost immediately a white security van appeared on my horizon racing towards me. I continued onwards but they maintained the same speed as myself, running parallel from their service road and I felt like a trespasser in their domain, against such resources employed versus such mutilation for the extraction of the chosen fuel for planet Earth.

The large site ended abruptly and the white van following my shadow turned back to continue their sentry role elsewhere. I was free of this artificial mechanical world and of the stalkers monitoring my journey through apocalyptic central.

Then a sign by the roadside stated "Speed enforced by aircraft" and right on cue a small Cessna airplane buzzed alongside the road in the distance checking speeds, does it mail a ticket in the post or does it swoop down to run you off the road? The main junction later had me turning right onto freeway 33, which was a dual carriageway but it afforded a nice wide smooth shoulder as protection and as we were getting close to the mountains the green fields got less and less to return to the familiar brown desert view.

This was a seriously dull road and to break the monotony I played music from the iPad from the handlebar bag, as the traffic was moderately light I allowed myself this luxury and this helped to raise the spirits, just make sure that the beat is right to encourage the cycling tempo.

I was helped by the music, weather and terrain to cruise along easily at 16mph, accompanied and powered by the beating sounds of *Status Quo* to *The Sweet*.

A couple of hours later and a large enclosed compound surrounded by wire and fences appeared on my left and this was the Avenal State Prison, a level 2 prison with 4,000 inmates under armed guard.

A massive penitentiary and a local employer just on the outskirts of the city of Avenal which as indicated on the city sign it is that it is the "Pistachio capital of the world" which provides the other main employment in the area. I decided to have a rest stop in Avenal so took the junction direct into the town centre where the 1935 art deco cinema dominates the buildings, making it look akin to the American town of Hill Valley in the "*Back to the Future*" film series.

I sat on a bench in the shade below a Pistachio tree watching the comings and goings of an American town whilst having some trail mix and a cold coke. It was all here, a bright yellow school bus and the classic police car outside the police station beside the all-way stop controlled junction; this was the archetypal small town America.

My bike had some admirers with one older chap impressed with the luggage system on the rack, he used to do some cycling when he was younger and commented that all he had was a rucksack and the pannier and rack pack system I was using was definitely an improvement, another plus was that he recognised I was English and not Australian.

I caught site of a sign by the side of a building that mentioned something about Valley fever with a picture of a concerned doctor in a white coat, I remembered seeing similar signs when up in Mojave, have I avoided the Valley Fever? What is it? Should I worry? Turns out that *"Coccidioidomycosis"* or Valley Fever is from a fungus found in the soil and when it rains the resultant mould is released into the air during activities such as farming, construction and interestingly during earthquakes. Just in California around 100 people a year die from it if the recipient has a low resistance to infections etc. I am lucky as there is no rain currently and even luckier as there has not been an earthquake.

Back onto the freeway to continue northwards to the coaling station or as it is now called, the town of Coalinga. When last week at 4.45pm in 1983, Coalinga was struck with a magnitude 6.5 earthquake which destroyed 300 homes and damaged thousands more including wiping out an 8-block commercial district, 64 people were injured and surprisingly only one person died of a consequential heart attack.

I eventually arrived at Coalinga and I cycled around the new commercial district that had been re-built after the earthquake with lots of information boards dotted around informing visitors to the stories and experiences from witnesses.

The motel was found which was a shame, as it was dreadful, the door which opened straight onto the road had a 2-inch gap below it allowing wind, fumes and probably rats into the room.

It was however cheap but not cheerful, too hot with non-functioning air-con and being right on the main road the trucks felt as if they were rumbling through the room. But, and this is what I kept telling myself, it has a bed which is off the floor so the cockroaches can keep themselves busy away from me. The TV worked on just two channels being Fox and NBC and the shower had just one channel being cold.

After nipping up the road to get dinner this was one place that I made sure that the bike was propped against the door after I closed it for the night, bike on guard during a very restless night as it was just far too loud for any proper sleep.

Ride Data	
Date	10/5/18
Cycling Distance (Miles)	62.11
Cycling Time (Hours)	5:56
Average speed (mph)	10.4
Elevation Gain (feet)	966

158

Chapter 24

Coalinga to King City

I was not upset to leave the motel, in fact I was ecstatic, after a grim night in the doppelganger of the Bates Motel it was time to go, the lack of sleep could be dealt with tonight, just put it down to experience for now. Today was going to be a hard one with 60 miles' duration and with nearly 4,000ft in climbs in the first 30 miles through rocky steep canyons.

Additionally, it was a straight through run with no civilisation such as shops anywhere on the route, I was on my own. A busy, twisty and narrow road with no shoulder was this morning's offering, I think it was being used as a cut through to Highway 101 from Interstate 5 for large trailer pulling trucks. It was not pleasant and I had to keep a close eye and ear to what was behind me in preparation to dive into any available space on the right. Fortunately, after the first valley there were major roadworks that required entering a convoy to pass.

This meant that I joined a queue of stationary traffic that had to wait for clearance to join behind the pilot car that led us through the roadworks.

When I passed the first traffic controller of the convoy she said to me "ride careful sir" and then she spoke on the radio to the driver in the pilot car letting him know that he was to drive slowly considering a bicycle being at the end of the convoy.

The roadworks lasted for about a mile with the top surface of the road ploughed up and replaced with lumpy and loose gravel, I was glad we were only moving slowly as the bike wanted to plough to the side and had to be constantly corrected. At the end of the convoy I thanked the pilot car driver for his courtesy and continued along the now tarmac road. The benefit of these roadworks for me was that the forced delay of 20 minutes waiting for the convoy meant that traffic coming up behind me was in waves. I heard the wave coming up and I pulled over knowing that the next wave was at least a full 20 minutes away.

This was a great way to own the road and this continued for the next few hours as I climbed up the on-going hills. The canyons became larger and deeper with steep almost sheer drops and the vegetation on them reduced to the occasional tree and bush.

These hills looked stark and aggressive with the road having to switch back and forth around them as it was just too steep. The number of ranches reduced the more barren the terrain became and one hill top ranch was set in a large dip in a hollowed-out mountain top. It looked like being inside a cone of an extinct volcano and this ranch located in the bottom must always be in the suns shadow, given that the rim was so far above.

This also felt like being in a massive empty stadium as there was no wind and no sound, as these too were blocked out by the massive brim.

I struggled to see where the road could escape this crater and then I saw that there was a split through the rocks on one side and that is where the road bent around at a sharp angle to exit the serene and stunning setting. In the exit portal both rock sides were sheer with recent rubble falls indicated along the side of the road, seeing these piles of scree made me speed up through these imposing natural gates, I did not want to be flattened under one of these massive bus-sized rocks.

At the halfway mark, I had cleared most of the climbing for the day and emerged on a road that had spent its time gripped to the side of the mountain which weaved and rose in a symbiotic sympathy of gradients. At the top, I once more met the San Andres fault line, which although invisible was still a bright red line through my map, just because I could not see it does not detract from its potential powerful influence to the region.

The hills all around me were created because of its powers; as the opposing tectonic plates were side swiping each other and forcing the earth's crust to form the local mountain ranges. The hills were thankfully still and quiet today although I know that one day standing in this location would be foolhardy and probably fatal but no-one knows in advance of when the next powerful earthquake will strike.

I then broke a record in the afternoon as I managed to get up to 45mph down the 3-mile-long hill with nice gentle sweeping bends.

My eyes were streaming, the helmet trying to lift off in the strong wind as I bunched right up whilst holding the drops for the most streamlined posture. It was great fun and very cooling, I even managed to avoid braking as the headwind ensured that I could not go any faster than this. The first peak had been conquered and just one more was left for today, in-between however was a valley filled with crops of all varieties soaking up the sun and being drip fed water from small hoses snaking around the field.

Some of these irrigation pipes were damaged and jets of water were being fired out creating a fine cooling mist that was being blown over the road, I just hoped that they did not contain pesticides.

I then saw a sign posted near the gate of a ranch that said "If you can read this sign you are within shooting range" I peddled quickly past that ranch. The trail mix I was carrying turned out to be inedible as I was unaware it had chocolate pieces in it and due to the heat, it had melted in the bag, the resultant mulch was gross and unfeasibly yucky and sticky. So once again bananas formed lunch with a side offering of Pringles washed down with warm coke.

Whilst enjoying this meal stop I checked over the bike as I had heard some ticking noises from the rear wheel whilst coming up the previous hill. I was mainly concerned with the spokes as they had had to contend with a lot of potholed roads and minor tracks.

The spokes all had good tension and the wheel still ran true, it turned out that the derailleur was just clipping the spokes when the camber of the road was extreme and exaggerating the dish of the rear wheel, so no worries, it was still good to go.

After waving greetings to a small procession of motorbikes that waved back enthusiastically, I re-joined the road. Then beside me on the dirt was another licence plate waiting to be found, this one was still attached to a front bumper so after a few screws were loosened I stashed this bent up Arizona plate with the other one in my growing collection. I am not sure if this is illegal but my philosophy is that it is recycling at its finest. Then the tarmac on the road disappeared completely which was a surprise but the dirt continued onwards. I cycled on although concerned that the entire road would soon stop. After about 2 miles the dirt got deeper and deeper so I had to start riding on the left of the road as the dirt was harder packed over there.

The dirt road was devoid of any traffic so that was not a problem. Eventually I heard a pick-up behind me so I moved back over to the right and as the pick-up went slowly past me I waved frantically at the driver. He stopped and it turned out he was the owner of the farm all around and that yes the tarmac road ahead does return in a few miles' time. He was very talkative and was surprised to meet a British cyclist who just happened to be cycling across his farm but he was happy to let me continue onto the main road.

We said cheerio and he quickly closed his window to return to the coolness of his air-con. The smooth tarmac road returned as promised so after another quick change to the right-hand side I continued along the valley.

The next smaller peak was traversed a little while later and I found myself in a massive agricultural valley that disappeared into the distance ahead and was flanked by mountain ranges at either side.

This valley contained the mighty USA Route 101 which is one of the main roads linking LA to San Francisco and all around a vibrant array of greens started to reflect in the sun ranging from lettuce's in the middle with vineyards around the edges. This was once again intensive farming but more crops from the ground such as lettuce and strawberries and less nut crops. The

Salinas River ran along the valley and at times it had a massively wide space to run although at this time of year it was just a small struggling brook using just a fraction of its available space, this was proven whilst crossing a long road bridge over the river bed.

The bridge was narrow and had no shoulder so I had to wait to access it when I was confident that no-one was behind me. I failed to realise the length of the bridge and about halfway across trucks started to fill my mirror behind me, there was no place for me to pull over so I had to continue although my pace had increased.

The trucks passed me, some giving me a wonderful wide berth but others sliced close to me as if to say "that's for holding me up". It was even more nerve racking when they overtook me on the bridge with a truck thundering the other way.

I would find out over the next few days that this was a pastime that some of the truck drivers employed to presumably pass the time, a sort of chicken and mouse game but I was the mouse. I fortunately made it to King City in one piece and luckily a restaurant and shop was perched right outside the motel.

Ride Data	
Date	11/5/18
Cycling Distance (Miles)	58.6
Cycling Time (Hours)	6:47
Average speed (mph)	8.6
Elevation Gain (feet)	3,707

Chapter 25

King City to Salinas

Saturday 12th May arrived and after an improved continental breakfast in reception it was time to pack up the bike making sure that I got the water out of the fridge at the last minute.

This motel was good as it was not one of the usual chains but owned and run by a family I met in reception last night. They were enthralled about my journey and asked lots of questions about the UK as they would like to visit it one day. They made sure that I had everything I needed in the room and even offered to drive me into town to go shopping if I wanted to, great honest people.

In fact, it was so good I recommend Keefers Inn, King City to anyone looking for a place to stay.

A 60-mile run today but less than 1,000ft of climbing so it should be a straightforward day, if only I knew what would develop later.

The road cut around the back of King City and flood warning signs were placed everywhere but it was bone dry. Perhaps these were from previous months during the snowmelt? I was not sure although it was clear that the river valley being very wide could have caused floods all along this flood plain. It's as if the road now knew this as it took a tangent up the side of the valley floor and gained altitude away from any potential floods.

I could see the 101 freeway in the distance and it was elevated on an earth bank as it traversed this low part of the valley floor. Strangely as I looked up the valley I could clearly see the hills in the distance either side but the head of the valley was obscured in a strange mist so I was unable to work out if my route would be up or down later in the day. The chosen path today was meandering in its direction; it reminded me of the Fens in Norfolk as I would go along in one direction then a 90 degree turn to the next turn of 90 degrees.

The fields had priority here and the roads had to accept their place around the outside, this allowed the fields to be ridiculously large. In the fields, there were a variety of crops at different stages of growth; one crop that was being harvested was lettuce.

A massive machine with a long spindly arm protruding outwards was where the workers sat and picked the green balls and after chopping off the excess they would put it in a conveyor belt in the middle of the spindle to go through to the main body part where they were being washed and then boxed.

It was an industrial process, around 20 people worked on the machine and parked all around the field were portable toilets and washing facilities positioned on trailers and powered by solar panels. Converted school busses were used to transport workers around the various picking sites.

In the Tamar Valley in Cornwall I had seen labour-intensive crop picking but here it was on a much grander scale and used technology to increase both the speed and efficiency. Waiting for them were the trucks with trailers that would ferry the produce onwards to arrive at its destination fresh for the consumer. I did try to make eye contact and perhaps start a conversation with some of these pickers but they were all wearing hoodies and avoided my gaze as if in a chain gang regime, I decided not to push my luck and possibly get them into trouble. I now went through Greenfield and deviated to the left of the valley where vineyards ran all along it, some offering indulgent tasting rooms that opened during the weekend, gosh that was now.

I was so tempted to try the Californian local wines but it would create two major problems, 1. Where could I store the bottles as I am sure they would want to sell it by the case and 2. Drinking wine or any alcoholic drink when riding a bike is just downright stupid.

At one point the GPS stated that I go straight on, the line of trees and total absence of a road dictated otherwise. Once this hiccup was negotiated in a 2 mile detour I was back on track. This happened again shortly afterwards and it appeared that the GPS was unable to tell the difference between a telegraph pole run and a road.

I threatened the GPS that if it continued to misdirect me it would be sacrificially thrown from the Golden Gate bridge into the Pacific in a few days' time!

Vineyard after vineyard went past me until it appeared that one major producer owned everything around the valley, as even the road signs were their own creation all showing the logo of this wine producer.

A small one-man helicopter in the distance was buzzing around checking the vines and even this had the familiar logo emblazoned on its side. The vines all had labels such as Cabernet Sauvignon, Chardonnay, Merlot and Pinot Noir attached to the end of the trellis.

I could feel my mouth salivating while imagining these rich bouquets, oak aromas and succulent tastes as I do like drinking a "new world" wine.

I stopped off at Gonzales to get a cold coke and whilst paying I spoke to the Asian-Indian shopkeeper and asked him why I was unable to see far down the valley. I had to repeat this a few times as he said that I spoke "British English and not American English" and "I would need to slow down" so he could understand me.

I was surprised that there was in fact a difference in these two dialects, I never considered it before. Anyway, it transpires that the mist at the valley head is the cool sea mist rolling in from the Pacific Ocean and it gets trapped and expands as it warms up once over the hot inland ground, it is something that local people have grown accustomed to seeing. It was, I am glad to say created neither by pollution or smog.

Leaving the small town on the aptly named Old Stage Road was a nice pleasant experience as it was quiet and sheltered from the growing wind. Unfortunately, this is when the day turned nasty, as around a few corners the full force of a 30-40mph headwind hit me hard, it must have been previously sheltered by the opposite mountain range but not anymore.

It was exhaustingly relentless without any gaps to take a break; I tucked down into the drops to reduce my opposition to it and went into a low gear. My speed dropped from an average of 12mph to around 7mph whilst using around 70% more energy to maintain even this slow speed. I calculated that the final 30 miles would take up to 5 hours even if I could maintain this painfully slow speed which I doubted was possible. Headwinds are always more demanding but this was incessant without stopping, it felt like I was cycling in a wind tunnel and I was getting drained fast.

As if this was not enough to affect my now downward mood the road although narrow and twisty had increasing amounts of traffic. I glanced over the valley to see that the 101 was still flowing which it was but the trucks for some reason have decided to deviate onto this microscopic road, perhaps they had heard on the CB radio that there was a mad English cycle tourer they could strife. It turned into open season of trucks versus cyclists, no quarter given, it was all out persecution. In the mirror, I could see a line of trucks behind and a line of trucks ahead, who would give first? Turns out no-one did apart from me, as in the last seconds before an imminent impact to the rear of my bike I acted with a lightning instinct and dived into the dirt field on the right. This probably saved my life and although my wheels dug into the dry deep powdery dirt stopping me instantly, I was still able to shout expletives and deliver the internationally known hand signal of "the bird" to the disappearing driver.

I had to carry out this manoeuvre two more times in the afternoon (the dive not the bird) which only made me more and more angry and feeling extremely vulnerable. My mood was low and became even lower after I failed to find an alternative route from this death road.

The headwind continued unabated to slow me down and draw out any remaining reserves of energy that I had. I would see a building beside the road and would pullup beside it to get a few minutes' calm away from the probing wind. I was close to quitting as both the natural elements and the traffic elements were all conspiring to destroy me in the shortest time possible, it was the most gruelling experience that I have ever found myself in whilst cycling, ever.

I was not even allowed to look at the scenery as full concentration was required to monitor the road. The thought of quitting was growing the harder the wind blew and the closer the trucks got, I was screaming at both the wind and the trucks but neither was listening, neither cared. Salinas seemed just too far to reach and I was not reducing the distance by much given the time it was taking.

If I quitted I would still be here, now and in the wind so I decided that it was pointless to even consider it as my lot would not improve in any way whatsoever. I had to try and find a mental safe-haven that I could reside in for the next few hours and luckily after turning onto Alisall Road the traffic density reduced as most went south to join the nearby 101.

I started to imagine cycling across the Golden Gate bridge and looking out over the bay to Alcatraz then chastising myself as I was worried a bit late in the day as there was only four days cycling left. If I was whimpish enough to quit then that should have taken place about a thousand miles ago, i.e. you're too later buster!

This mental argument lasted quite a while with neither side backing down. Then I got to Salinas city before I knew it, my head battle had got me through it. I was met in the hotel by a husband and wife team that were so

171

happy and cheerful in stark contrast to my current mood. They were funny and relaxed and cracking jokes; they should have been doing a double act in Vegas. They were concerned to hear my story of the traffic crammed road and they said that some trucks have started to use the small road to avoid the police check-points that sometimes spring up on the 101 over the weekend.

I was allocated my room and as soon as I opened the door it was super cool and comfortably furnished and once again just next door was an assortment of food outlets, as I was so depleted of energy I decided for my best health interests was to have a meat based meal and not a vegetarian replacement. It did the trick as I felt physically and mentally recharged afterwards.

A slight concerned niggle still flowed around my thoughts and that was the issue of the destructive headwind. I could not tolerate that amount of punishment again; if it did return I was worried that it could destroy my last few days cycling. I understood given the direction I was taking that the prevailing wind would generally be ahead of me, I just hoped that today's demonstration was extreme and not just the ordinary.

Ride Data	
Date	12/5/18
Cycling Distance (Miles)	60.69
Cycling Time (Hours)	6:32
Average speed (mph)	9.3
Elevation Gain (feet)	940

Chapter 26

Salinas to Gilroy

Welcome to Mother's Day in USA which is two months after the UK version, on an overcast and cool day. I was so pleased that I did not give up yesterday even at my lowest ebb I managed to forge through.

From now on the rides are not too remote and there will be small towns that I can stop at for food and supplies. Although I am close to the Californian coast I will be heading further inland today in a dog leg shaped route. This is because the most direct road is only the 101 which does not allow bicycles. I will need to go over the mountain peak towards Hollister and then take a sharp left towards Gilroy.

I head off in an easterly direction to conquer the Vierra Canyon via the San Juan Grade Road. The terrain has turned into a cross between Devon and New Zealand with large grassy hills and peaks with cattle grazing along the sides of the canyon. Then at the junction with Crazy Horse Canyon Road, trucks are prohibited to continue over the hills and must turn left on Crazy Horse road, as the road ahead is just a narrow twisty steep road. That was great to see as going over this hill I did not have to worry with trucks looming up behind me whilst climbing the 1,000ft high canyon.

I had the road essentially to myself on this Sunday morning and on the climb, I even had to put on my light cycling jacket as it was turning cold. The road swept left then right, swooping up a hill and trickled down a little before resuming upwards. This roller coaster continued upwards and got very steep, so steep that I decided to get off and walk a little which was refreshing. I could look better around me at the amazing green and hilly scenery, some bits looking like the *Hobbits "Shire"* from *The Lord of the Rings*, which had increasing numbers of cattle grazing standing steadfast on the sides of very steep hills looking as steady as mountain goats.

I continued my walk upwards feeling my calf muscles complaining from the unusual activity of pushing a heavy bike up a hill.

The gradient reduced so I got back on the bike and immediately my calf felt better back doing the tasks it had got used to over the last one thousand or so miles.

A few more sharp corners and I had ascended the hill and was at its peak and only one car had passed me so far. Ahead the green San Benito county line sign indicated that a change in local authority was ahead, however to reinforce this change the actual road surface changed colour and became rough and potholed right below the sign. So, workers who maintain the road must get to the county line on the Salinas county side and stop, "Well that's San Benito's problem now, tools down lads it's time to go home" they must say.

The road was awful and downright dangerous requiring a zig-zagging action to constantly miss wheel buckling lumps and bumps, once again I was glad that I had the road virtually to myself as I was all over the place. I took a break from the teeth jangling ruts and used *Facetime* to talk to home and catch up on things whilst having a snack of chocolate free trail mix. I could see down the hill fully from here and below me was the town of San

Juan Bautista looking affluent and exclusive with massive gardens or yards as they are called in America, spreading out around each property. A well-manicured clean looking golf course with bright sand bunkers was also running alongside the well-heeled town.

It was a bumpy descent, making sure that the speed remained low as the road surface was disgusting and just one badly hit rut could buckle a wheel easily. At the valley floor, I had to join the only road through to Hollister which was a main road being the 156 which after seeing a couple of Sunday cycle club riders whizzing past on their super light carbon fibre rockets gave me confidence to ride it. It did have a nice shoulder but it was jammed with fast moving ear-shattering traffic just a few feet away from me.

It was grim cycling and roads like this give an indication why cycling in this part of California is frowned upon as dangerous and foolhardy. The infrastructure for cyclists apart from a line of paint in the cities is virtually the only compromise provided and in the remote out of town areas there is nothing, if it was not for the shoulders which tend to be part of most USA roads anyway, cycling in those areas would be impossible.

Looking ahead I am not sure if there is any impetus to improve upon the status quo either as there is just not the volume of complaining cyclists demanding it.

After traversing the city of Hollister in the now strong sunlight, I had to double back on refreshing minor roads to head north to Gilroy. On the horizon looking northwest there was a strange white cloud formation rolling low over the hills, looking like surf coming over a beach, this was the clouds being formed from the cold Pacific meeting the warmer mountains such as Mt Madonna Peak and Twin Peaks West.

It was an impressive sight especially realising that just behind this anomaly was near to my final destination. On the road, the smells from the fields was becoming overpowering which was from the garlic crops, not an unpleasant smell but it takes some getting used to.

Gilroy is the world's garlic capital and celebrates this every July; in fact this year will be the 40th such event. There is a garlic theme throughout Gilroy such as the world famous delicious garlic ice cream? and the crowning of Miss Gilroy Garlic Festival Queen.

Beside the road were many different coloured post-boxes of a multitude of shapes, some with flags on their lids and others just open to the elements. They were all bunched together and next to a layby, which I surmised was due to a different method than that employed in the UK.

As most houses have large front gardens and some are miles off the main road the post office delivers to the post-box and not the house, I assume this is quicker and easier for the delivery man. I did recall seeing a solitary post-box in the Mojave Desert that was the only sign of any civilisation for miles around, so the house must have been many more miles distant from its post box off the highway. Also, some streets had the post boxes on just one side of the street regardless of what side of the road they lived, again this is to streamline the delivery system from the little white vans they use, as stopping on just one side is far more economical than stopping on both sides. Interestingly the white US Post Office vans are the biggest civilian fleet of vehicles of any corporation in the world and I think they look a bit like postman Pat vans.

Ride Data	
Date	13/5/18
Cycling Distance (Miles)	42.28
Cycling Time (Hours)	4:33
Average speed (mph)	9.3
Elevation Gain (feet)	1,221

179

Chapter 27

Gilroy to Santa Clara

Watching the news on the TV on the wall of the breakfast room I mentioned to the only other guest that the number of adverts on the TV was insane.

As all channels in the US are the same she asked why UK television was different. When I said that for the BBC we all paid a licence fee so there are no adverts, she thought that was a bad idea after I told her how much we paid.

We chatted about the cyclist's lot in California and she said that she would never consider riding a bike around as it looks far too dangerous and that once over the age of 13 when you can no longer ride on the sidewalk you should be banned from the road. I decided not to pursue the shortfalls of her argument so I bid farewell and got the bike ready.

As soon as I started on the road I had to stop as it felt chilly, so once again I donned the cycling jacket to keep warm. Although my desired direction is north my path meandered around to avoid the high volume main roads. The valley was still my companion for today as I followed its path towards the fog flowing in from the bay area of San Francisco.

It was interesting to see that the more urban the area the greater the number of cyclists, together with the unwanted element of cyclists who feel that going against the traffic, running red lights and generally being a pain to everyone came out. I found myself passing through many residential areas with hidden cut-throughs that would never exist on a paper map; the GPS was cleverly navigating a nice quiet path. Even going down roads where I felt that there would be a dead-end turned out to have an exit of sorts that allowed me to continue along very sleepy roads. The GPS was clearly trying to impress me today, probably considering my recent threat.

The residential areas always had about three-quarters of the houses equipped with a white flag pole angled out from the front porch with the stars and stripes flag being patriotically flown. Likewise, around businesses it was a competition to have the biggest flag flying or if that was not possible then have half a dozen flying instead. I was very much off the beaten track seeing hidden areas such as small parks, memorials and other civic amenities that flowed past me on my transit through.

Then a few hours later the well-marked cycle paths returned painted in shocking green, I had entered the district of San Jose.

I had my own lane and space around me which made for a much more relaxed cycling. The area of Silicon Valley was around me with its hi-tech businesses positioned in modern buildings with manicured lawns all around. The route took me through the centre of the San Jose State University with its familiar facilities of library, lecture theatres and student support services that I had been involved in during my own career in the UK whilst lecturing at college in Plymouth.

The one obvious difference was the armed security guards milling around the campus but they looked less menacing than other armed security I had seen in other locations. Lots of students were chilling in-between lectures and there was an air of optimism, in an area that has been so influential in the global digital revolution that we all benefit from, these were the future captains of industries that in some cases have not yet been invented. Students were also scooting around the campus on electric scooters which appear to be everywhere, they can be hired via your phone and once activated you can use them for the hire period. Once finished with they are left on the street where they get collected overnight and charged ready for the following day.

As a cyclist, the problem is that electric scooters are quick and some of the riders ignore the rules of the road and thus become another threat that should be monitored. Sharing a cycle path with other bikes can be difficult enough and once you add into that mix electric scooters by individuals or I have seen two people on one at the same time, it starts to become a recipe for disaster. Although the law states that scooter riders must wear helmets, no-one does, also most riders wear two earphones or actual headphones whilst riding blocking out all sounds, again the law in California is that no more than one earphone must be worn by road users for obvious safety reasons. Additionally, traffic must give cyclists at least 3 feet of room when passing and if there is insufficient space such as narrow roads or on-coming traffic then they must wait behind until it's clear.

That's the written and legal definition; its application however is virtually the opposite.

The answer is in active enforcement; however, I have yet to see this in action on either side of the pond.

Then my shoulder pain returned as if a sharp knife had sliced through my shoulder blade, it was agonising. I had to take some pain killers which in my humble opinion do nothing for me, so I also topped up this approach with some anti-inflammatory tablets that I had brought with me from the UK.

I cycled steady for the next hour waiting for them to kick in and stopping every few miles to exercise the shoulder to try and ease the pain. Surprisingly all my efforts were in vain as the pain continued unabated, I just had to deal with it mentally. I started to visualise what I had seen and done so far in a relatively short space of time on this cycle tour. Also, I considered the other tours that I had done and remembered all the amazing places and people that I had seen in other countries and on balance a bit of shoulder pain was a small price to pay for such experiences and the incredible travelling freedom that cycle touring allows. Then I had another thought that the freedom of cycling has always allowed me to see a country truthfully and not a sanitised version that would be seen if only its major attractions were visited and traversed in a car or a plane.

This was my penultimate day's ride and it was now nearing completion, I could see the Motel 6 across the road from a tyre garage with the most amazing sized American flag flapping in the wind, it was so large that the flagpole was bending with the weight. Check-in was straightforward assisted by the helpful Helen who was keen to make sure that everything was adequate and she added that if the room was not suitable for the bike they would gladly change it for another one. Once in the room

I asked the bike if it was acceptable but surprisingly it offered no comment either way.

Ride Data	
Date	14/5/18
Cycling Distance (Miles)	45.05
Cycling Time (Hours)	4:15
Average speed (mph)	10.6
Elevation Gain (feet)	332

Chapter 28

Santa Clara to San Francisco

This motel only offered coffee in the morning as an additional perk and as a non-coffee drinker I thus went thirsty. Not to worry, as I stopped off at the Mc Donald's for a pancake breakfast with a cold fruit juice, which although sickly does set the calories for the day.

Today on my journey to the Golden Gate Bridge I would be cycling alongside the San Francisco Bay, probably first seen by Europeans in 1579 whilst sailing on Sir Francis Drake's circumnavigation of the globe.

The bay is a massive inland area which size has been affected over the centuries by the varying uses of mining, industries and farming in this area of California.

As I started up the left spit of land between the bay and the Pacific Ocean, space becomes less available and this resulted in more compact living spaces. This squeezing also brings main roads closer to communities and communities closer to industry.

Over seven million people live in the towns and cities that surround the bay area and the resultant criss-crossing bridges over the bay have been built to cope with the growing traffic movements for both individuals and businesses alike to thrive.

At the time of writing California State now has a greater GDP (Gross Domestic Product) than the entire UK, it is without a doubt the main powerhouse of the USA, even more surprising is that the state's population of 36 million compares to the UK's 65 million. Now heading north close to Palo Alto and Stanford University the history of this area brings up familiar names such as *Apple, Google, Facebook, Logitech* and *PayPal*. These are all household names that have been so influential in the lives of everyone on the planet, be it in social media, the Internet, Electronic Commerce with associated payment systems and hardware to link it all together.

As a previous lecturer specialising in electronic communications, I could relate to how these industries and their remarkable innovations have allowed every one of us to have real time information and communications, which just 25 years ago would have seemed impossible.

I saw the first road bridge across the bay being the Dumbarton Bridge carrying the Route 84 highway; this was also the only bay bridge that you can cycle across in its entirety to Newark. It was a low bridge with a hump in the middle to allow small boats underneath; no large vessels would make it this far south in the shallow waters of the bay.

Next I cycled past Redwood City getting closer to the bay all the time and within earshot of the mighty freeways of the 101 and the 82 carrying thousands of vehicles both in and out of the pinch point of San Francisco City ahead. The next bridge across is the San Mateo Bridge which carries the US 92 and is elevated across on stilts with a much larger hump in the middle to Hayward City.

This bridge at 7 miles long is the longest in California and was reinforced in 1997 to withstand earthquakes especially after the fatal 1989 Loma Prieta quake. My route was now getting difficult to follow as the cycle routes and paths were not signposted at all and I was reliant on the small screen on the GPS to navigate around and across large streets and often around or under freeways. Then close to San Francisco Airport I was instructed to go north over a flyover and pick up the cycle path turning left.

I proceeded over the flyover which was akin to Long Beach traffic levels and intensity which had me trudging up the incline slowly with traffic passing within mere inches. I looked over the top of this flyover for the cycle path entrance at its base but all I could see was the on ramp for the US 101 with its constant stream of traffic, this was clearly no place for any cyclist if they wanted to survive the day.

I had to decide what to do whilst there was still a small sidewalk available, do I continue or turn around? After a short while I realised that this would be the third time that I had come across this predicament and so perhaps third time lucky would help me. I wrestled the bike onto the sidewalk and returned down the flyover to the previous path that I had been on. This I then followed on a parallel direction to the phantom path in the hope that our paths would cross soon.

The air traffic around me became busier as more and more planes were landing and taking off, again in a tandem method using the side by side runways in the city centre airport. The runways are built right out into the bay itself and a long line of pins were sticking out the water beyond them to mark the approach to the runway. This airport has a troubled past with near and actual catastrophes with the most recent occurring in 2017 when an Air Canada A320 nearly landed at night on a taxi-way after mistaking it for the main runway. Fortunately, the tower instructed them to go around at the last minute avoiding a crash on the taxi-way with five fully laden planes carrying over one thousand people. If the landing had continued it is obvious to all that this would have become the world's worst air disaster.

Then back in 2013 a landing Boeing 777 with Asiana Airlines carrying 300 passengers hit the seawall prior to the runway and the resultant fuselage break up killed 3 passengers and injured 50. This crash was attributable to pilot error by approaching the airport at too steep an angle and additionally ignoring the many instruments informing them of this worsening situation. Interestingly two of the passengers killed were later proven to be not wearing their seat belts upon landing, if they had worn them experts believe that they could of walked away from the crash unharmed.

Best not to dwell on these I thought, as I would be flying from here in less than a week's time. Then at St Bruno after crossing the busy 101 I saw in the distance another cyclist that seemed to know where they were going. He turned down what I thought was a dead-end to the side of an off-ramp, I followed behind hoping that I was wrong and when I got to the same point I could see that there was a gap in the fence and a small sign pointed out that this was the San Francisco Bay Trail route.

This would take me north on a mixture of bike only paths and on-road shared paths. Its first job was to take me underneath the interstate 380 and its on-off ramps in a derelict piece of land that now had a major new use, a massive tent city. It was vast and filled the entire space available beside the trail, with an assortment of small home-made tents to larger family tents and some shelters made from plastic and tarpaulin.

These all converged around the rubbish strewn and foul smelling small river course that wound its way into the bay. I once again had to remind myself that I was next to San Francisco airport, one of the busiest international airports and not a slum in a developing nation. The shock of contrasts and perceived acceptance of poverty was again difficult for me to understand, who was supporting this transient tent city to move on and find a more permanent housing solution? It was sad to see the lives of whole families living cheek by jowl and physically close to the American dream but separated by a vast distance of legal status and rights to stay.

This transient town was one of the sights that I will always remember as it is a physical demonstration of when humans get it wrong, totally and recklessly. No one seems to take responsibility or act morally to first improve the occupant's lives and then eradicate these slums from ever needing to be built again. I have seen this before played out in a variety of different countries such as in Africa, the UK and now in America, it needs resolving by our politicians and leaders.

Then the mighty Bay Bridge came into view, a massive grey double decker road bridge that swooped across the bay and sank its anchor into Yerba Buena Island next to Treasure Island before starting again for the shoreline of Oakland city. Its height was staggering together with the amount of traffic that was moving swiftly across its metal floored lanes, producing a reverberating and clunking harmony of rubber on steel. The skyscrapers of San Francisco city were now growing bigger ahead of me, with a mix assortment of concrete and steel constructions in this earthquake capital of the western seaboard USA. Then there were the hills which were steep and everywhere as I remembered from the old 1970's TV cop show of the *Streets of San Francisco*.

The cycle paths merged back into the main traffic lanes so I had to learn to fight for space once again and become more aware of everything around me to respond promptly. My original plan was to go straight to the hotel and visit the Golden Gate and other attractions tomorrow, however the weather today was clear without the fog that often blankets both the bridge and the bay area so I decided that it would be prudent to continue these visits today.

I did not want to go and see the bridge tomorrow and find it draped in fog, so now seemed the better solution. The GPS was programmed to take me to Pier 39 being the northerly point of the city by the bay so I could follow the estuary around to meet the Golden Gate Bridge.

A new threat also appeared on the road and that was from trolley busses that either had normal wheels but linked to an overhead power source or had train wheels and had to follow the tracks. These tracks were the main concern as they ran parallel to the path and as we all know if you get a wheel trapped in a track grove it spells certain disaster. I ran wide of these dangers which made my position along the road wider, much to the obvious dislike of other traffic that continued to harass and beep at me.

Then at major junction's new designs of traffic signals appeared for the bus and tram drivers to follow which only added to the chaos and confusion.

The roads were now visually busy with a rich assortment of distractions be it the mass of high voltage wires above the roads for the trolley busses to draw power from, to the occasional green bike sign painted on the roads and the red painted full lane marked "taxi bus only" signs. Rails sunk into the road were the worst distraction of all and ignored at your peril. I was busy both mentally and physically and it was a great feeling, it's amazing how quick you get accustomed to the road dynamics of a new city even if it is on the other side of the world.

The skyscrapers were now all around me, such as the iconic 1972 white concrete Transamerica Pyramid standing at 850 feet, to the tallest and virtually brand new 1,070 feet high total glass Salesforce tower. Which has at its peak a nine-story electronic work of art which is due to be commissioned and activated in a week's time, unfortunately I will be back in the UK when this occurs. The massive 1,800 feet Sutro TV tower on Mount Sutro with its three prongs rising skywards in the shape of a trident was becoming as much a part of the scenery around me as the Bay Bridge and the imposing skyscrapers. I then cut beside China town on my journey north avoiding street cars, scooters and busses all coming from different angles, to at least unnerve me and at worse squash me.

Then the bay-side area was ahead of me just on the other side of the famous Embarcadero which separated the piers on the waterfront to the city streets inland. I followed the bike only traffic lights and crossed over to the bright green cycle path to arrive at Pier 39, which was a buzzing and vibrant tourist attraction in San Francisco.

It was busy with hordes of people, so I walked the bike along the pier looking at the variety of stores and restaurants such as *Bubba Gump Shrimp Co*, *Hard Rock Café*, and even a fish and chip shop. Then looking over the side I could clearly see Alcatraz Federal Penitentiary glinting in the bright sunlight.

This rock is well known for its prison history from 1934 to 1963 where contrary to popular films no-one has ever escaped alive from its confines. It was closed in 1963 due to its running and upkeep costs which were three times as much as other land based high security prisons. It is now a tourist attraction where you can get a ferry over and see how life in the prison was; I also read that you can be locked into a famous gaol to experience it for yourself, albeit for a few minutes only.

At the far end of Pier 39 are the floating pontoons that are frequented by the sunbathing and barking sea lions that can be viewed from a safe distance. Watching their bulbous shapes emerge from the sea to sunbath on the pontoon unaware of the constant clicking from photographs being taken by the waiting audience. Unfortunately, it was time to move on so I pushed the bike back down through the busy Pier 39 to the Embarcadero and had my first full glimpse of the Golden Gate Bridge in the distance and it was epic.

I was now being drawn to my symbolic finish point just a few miles away but first I had to follow the bay around to meet it. On the way, I came across the Palace of Fine Arts Theatre, a Greco-Roman palace built for the 1915 Panama- American exposition, this version was a re-built copy of the original which after all was only built to stand for the duration of the exposition only. Across the road in Crissy Field the cycle path ran right beside the beach providing a panoramic view of the Golden Gate Bridge which was now tantalisingly close.

I stopped having a cold coke and a chat to several tourists who like me where seeing the iconic bridge for the first time. I mentioned that I was soon going to cycle across it which they responded with a hint of envy. They needn't of as many of their fellow tourists were hiring bikes from hire companies to undertake the journey themselves, this I discovered as most of my fellow-cyclists were ill-equipped and weaving from side to side as if riding a bike for the first time.

I then spotted another great vantage point to take that all important selfie, which I was about to do when a chap lying on the bench opposite sat up and said Hi. His bike was beside him so as a fellow cyclist I asked if he wouldn't mind taking a picture of me and my bike in front of the Golden Gate Bridge. He sprang into action, took my camera after a brief lesson and started to take several pictures, although he clearly had a flair for the dramatic.

One picture he took of me whilst he was lying on the ground, another he climbed up a wall to get the "extra height" as he called it. Finally, he verbally moved an entire group of people out of the shot before returning my camera to me in a triumphant mood, it was weird but fun.

The path continued to underneath the Golden Gate Bridge stopping at Fort Point, a civil war fort located in a strategic point of the "golden gate" entrance to the bay, hence its name. This was a dead end but I stopped and spent some time watching the breakers come washing over the boundary wall; some went crashing over without warning and soaked the occasional child that tried to play chicken with the sea.

Looking at the underneath of the bridge gave me a full idea of the scale of the world's longest bridge from 1937 until 1964. The weather conditions were perfect with a bright blue clear sky with the temperature in the mid-twenties, little wind and of most importance no fog anywhere.

I retraced my path back to the steep hill upwards that would take me to the Golden Gate trail, this I took cautiously as it was a tricky gradient together with the novice cyclists zig-zagging all over the path.

At the top, we then merged with the busy pedestrian traffic so I crawled along making sure that my heavy bike did not hit any unsuspecting jaywalkers. The path then used a small tunnel under the main bridge deck and at this point only cyclists could continue onto the west side of the bridge, pedestrians were directed to the east side only.

I was getting more excited at this point as only a few hundred feet remained of my quest which had been planned in detail all those months before and here I am completing what I thought was possibly achievable but known to be downright difficult. I turned the corner and I was on the far left of the bridge following the cycle path, a few inches to my right was the roadway that had traffic heading towards me.

The most noticeable thing was the noise of the tyres going over the metal expansion strips and making a "ha-ha-he-he" reverberating metallic sound, and judging that the lower the pitch the larger the vehicle going over it. It was a constant ear splitting background noise; this was the reality of the working bridge being a workhorse for travel and is not something you consider when romanticising about visiting the Golden Gate Bridge. I found the quietest part to pull over and call home from this famous location although it was difficult for both sides to hear much of the conversation with six lanes of traffic fully occupied.

The views out across the Pacific were amazing and below me was a constant flow of both commercial and pleasure craft flowing both in and out of the bay. I reached the half way point and as always this is the most noticeable part of any suspension bridge to feel the swing and the undulations caused by the heavy traffic and wind. It was gently swaying and then lunged when a truck went over the middle portion only to return to a gentle sway again. Up close it is painted a reddish orange in colour and not golden, the "golden gate" refers to the physical harbour mouth and not the colour of the bridge.

The colour orange was chosen as it is the most noticeable by boats navigating the waters below in the dense fog that often covers this area. The construction was industrial in its appearance with some one million rivets plus used to construct the two piers and the roadway, with 27,000 wires bundled together to make the two-main cable stays, again all painted in the same striking colour. Bicycles were sign posted to do no more than 15mph which was being ignored by the cyclists coming down the hill of the arch so I had to be cautious when navigating the narrow pier parts of the bridge, I had made it this far the last thing I wanted was a crash especially involving another cyclist.

At the end, I turned around and made my way back southbound only to see a very strange vehicle coming up the middle of the bridge traffic lanes. A bright yellow oblong box on wheels called the "Road Zipper" was crawling along and moving the central barrier from one lane to the other to increase the number of lanes going northbound. Apparently, this activity happens many times a day to increase/decrease the number of lanes in a direction based on traffic densities. Our local suspension bridge over the River Tamar only has 3 lanes and has overhead lights to do that task at a flick of a switch, here they must run the road zipper through end to end to get the same result.

Many more cyclists joined me southbound as I suspected they had cycled the pedestrian/cycle east side of the bridge first and were returning on the west side. I was bumbling along slowly in comparison due to the weight of the bike and I was also taking in the experience and then into the mix came the commuter cyclists that did not care for any speeds below 20mph, so it was chaos at the pinch points or where other tourists just stopped to take that important picture. I experienced the verbal road rage by the other cyclists which did feel a little intimidating, after all if I can't fit through I will wait until I can, that's the philosophy of the last 1,100 miles and it served me well so far, so "wait up buddy" was my reply.

At the southern pier, a couple were on the side of the path looking at one of their bikes and scratching their heads, it was clear that the chain had disappeared down between the cassette and wheel beside the spokes.

I asked if they wanted any help and their relived faces indicated that yes they did.

They were using hired bikes so had no tools with then, we had a quick chat and they agreed that cycling the bridge was a once in a lifetime bucket list experience even with the constant traffic noise and fumes spreading out from the road. I took out my tool roll and as it was chain work I put on the disposable gloves as I hate chain grease staining my fingers for days at a time. Top-tip, always carry some disposable gloves in the tool kit; they will always come in handy. The small pliers helped grab the chain wedged down the gap and combining pulling and turning the back wheel allowed me to re-engage the chain on the cassette. Then to stop it happening again I turned the stop screw a few turns for good measure. It turned out that they were from San Diego which is south of LA and that they chose to cycle over the bridge in place of one of the other favourite tourist methods which is to hire a three wheeled *Gocar,* a bright plastic wedged shaped mini car. These take two people and have GPS guidance with a storytelling audio soundtrack all in a bond-buggy lookalike vehicle.

Looking at these buzzing around the mean streets of San Francisco and struggling to reach the top of some of the hills I think that they made the correct healthier choice. We said farewell to each other and they wobbled off to continue their memory making journey.

I looked over the bridge for one last time before cycling off it and I recounted the experiences on my journey thus far, even though this was my quest's symbolic journey end I knew that USA cycling had a few more days to go and anyway there will be other quests in the future for me to undertake. The GPS was re-adjusted to take me to my rather expensive hotel for tonight and within the hour I had arrived at the Queen Anne, a Victorian hotel. A quick shower later I was back in the drawing room downstairs sipping the complimentary sherry and devouring the delicious cookies and chatting to a couple from Norway.

The hotel room was done out in a Victorian style of garishness in the flowerily bedspread with gold curtains and matching wallpaper, it was busy to the eye but the bike was allowed in so I could relax knowing the bike would still be there in the morning. I popped out for a salad dinner from a deli around the corner where the Italian chef was talking to me about the current news around the world cup and agreeing about the disappointment of Italy not qualifying for the first time since 1958, and how much poorer the world cup will be as a result.

Back in the hotel room I watched the news saying that there had been an earthquake yesterday in the Oakland area with a magnitude of 3.5, my mate Neil in Walnut

Creek had felt it and had said to me that it was the biggest shake they had had for a few years. Also as a precaution the Bay Area Rail Transit (BART) has suspended trains pending track inspections. This was all due to deep ground movement in the Haywood fault and not from the well-known San Andres Fault.

Ride Data	
Date	15/5/18
Cycling Distance (Miles)	63.15
Cycling Time (Hours)	7:03
Average speed (mph)	9
Elevation Gain (feet)	1,775

Chapter 29

San Francisco to Walnut Creek

Luckily, I felt no quakes overnight and the ground was suitably still when I had a massive pile of scrambled eggs on toast for breakfast, washed down with litres of fruit juice. I was totally full of food when I left the hotel for my last cycling day over to Walnut Creek but first I wanted to visit the famous steep twisty Lombard Street and see the iconic San Francisco cable cars.

I entered Lombard Street into the GPS and followed the route up and down some very steep and scary hills which make up downtown San Francisco.

One hill I went down looked straight out over the water to Alcatraz Island with passenger ferries darting back and forth to it.

As Lombard Street is a steep one way hill down, I knew that the ride to its start would be a trudge uphill and I was not disappointed, it was a killer climb. At the top of Lombard Street with the road below me there were pedestrian tourists everywhere watching and photographing the cars start their perilous journey down the 27 percent incline with 8 sharp bends. This bendy road has appeared in many films and as such is well known.

I lined up and the expectant crowd were surprised to see a fully laden bike undertake the challenge, I heard comments like "hope your brakes are good bud" and "it's far too steep, does he know what he is doing?". Final brake check complete I slowly descended the red bricked road keeping the descent speed under check, it was not as bad as I thought, in fact many coastal roads leading down to hidden fishing harbours in Cornwall are far worse, although having my photograph taken many times on the descent was new.

The corners were sharp but I still had enough room to sweep around them whilst maintaining the same speed, the brakes were holding the speed firm so no problems experienced. I did note the hedge around the outside which would have been my dive zone if the need arose. I think the crowd were disappointed that I had cleared the steep part without any mishaps. I stopped at the junction below to take some pictures and a couple from Canada came over and offered to take my picture for me.

We got chatting about their visit and its highlights so far and how they had done some cycle touring in their younger days and were considering going back to it. They were interested about my trip and its successful completion and they were eager to look at my trip details on my website when they got back to their hotel. They took some great pictures of me standing in front of Lombard Street which I could never have done on my own.

Next I was going to track down a vintage cable car at the manual turntable located at Hyde Street, as this is down by the wharf it was downhill all the way, making sure that I avoided any of the tracks buried in the road.

At Hyde Street, a cable car was just leaving with passengers hanging onto the outside as is customary even though there are plenty of seats inside the car.

The cable car system here in San Francisco is the world last functioning manual cable car system running, which started taking passengers in 1873. They function by gripping a running steel cable buried under the road to move forward and it is released to stop it being driven. To stop, the brakes on the car act to slow the wheels.

The cable cars now operate on just a few remaining routes as these courses contained hills too steep for the electric replacements to climb.

Now it is mainly a tourist attraction and not a viable method to commute around the city.

The manual turn-table is just that, a turntable that the car is pushed onto and manually spun around so it is now facing the other way, it is then pushed off ready to engage the cable when it wants to move forward. I watched this happen and it appeared that only the slightest push by the conductor was sufficient to both move the car and spin it around.

When it was ready a new crowd of passengers rushed on quickly and took prime positions on the outside grab rail to be whisked up the hill whilst having the full wind in your face experience. One chap had his selfie stick so far out in front it looked like he was a jouster riding into battle. The Embarcadero cycle path was picked up to go south towards the ferry pier but I turned off early as in the port was a massive cruise ship called the Grand Princess and flowing out of the pier was an assortment of taxis, busses and coaches transporting the 3,000 passengers off the ship.

The sidewalk which I was now walking down was being controlled by a couple of police officers to allow traffic in and out. The jovial officers asked me to wait to allow a few coaches out onto the Embarcadero which I gladly did, when the sidewalk was clear they happily allowed us through however, the traffic on the road was in a state of total gridlock. Car horns blasted, trucks honked but no-one was going anywhere, put an emptying cruise ship in a busy city and I suppose this is what happens. I glided nicely along the bright green cycle path amongst the cacophony of sounds, shall I ring my bell to add to the mayhem? better not I thought. I was looking for the pier that housed the ferries going to Oakland which I believed was number 14, I knew that pier 39 was north so I was checking the big numbers posted on each pier as I headed south but it was not making any sense. I found out later that the pier numbers north of the ferry building are odd numbers and even numbers south of it. I do not understand the reasoning behind this but now I was so confused that I resorted to cycling south to see what would transpire.

I continued along the path and noted that the traffic was now easing so I could relax a little bit as the chance of a rogue car driving up the cycle path was diminishing. I arrived at a large pier building which I believed was the ferry building so I pushed the bike in amongst the stalls and shops that were inside the arched atrium.

For an old historic ferry building it looked like a shopping centre, which was very busy as well, tables and chairs by cafés with diners dining and bars with drinkers drinking and I had to navigate a wide heavy and unwieldly bike amongst them. I looked a bit of a plonker to be honest and out of place with my surroundings. "Where do I buy a ticket for the ferry?" I asked many people with blank responses when at last; one person gave me proper directions to the ticket sales counter which was hidden inside a shop. The one-way ticket was $9 and the bike was free however, I would have two hours to kill as I had just missed one ferry to Oakland. I got a cold drink and waited outside on a bench when a chap turned up with a shopping trolley full of his worldly belongings, he produced a six pack of beers and offered me one, I said no as I was cycling over to Walnut Creek after the ferry but thanked him for his generosity, which on the face of it would probably be equivalent to me offering him my car.

We had a great chat and he was a very unassuming man that was clearly down on his luck but he felt that this was only going to be temporary and things would soon improve. After he finished his first can of beer he gathered his belongings and said "Catch you later Englishman" as he trundled away. This bench afforded a great view of the Bay Bridge and I could hear the traffic rumbling through both levels, beyond that in the distance was the city of Oakland on the other side of the bay and behind that was the rising peaks of Berkeley.

The large catamaran ferry arrived and moored up on the pontoon and we all went aboard, I found the large cycle storage racks and noted only one other bike out of possible spaces for about 20. I secured the front wheel into the clamp and went upstairs to the stern of the ferry outside.

I was quickly joined by Theresa who was the owner of the other touring bike on the ferry, she was cycling solo to Mexico stopping with hosts and camping along the way. We exchanged stories of our trips and discussed the

204

differences of her American touring bike of choice being the Surly versus the Dawes I was riding. I also looked aft to see the city of San Francisco disappearing behind me with its iconic skyline and selection of bridges and islands. We talked bike touring speak across the bay and before we knew it we had arrived at the dockside of Oakland. I wished her well and safe travels as we departed for our separate ways, I was heading north she went west.

The nice green cycle path paint was now just a memory and I was thrown into the mire once again. Oakland was not as wealthy as the suburbs of San Francisco and I remember that this is where a few riots had started in the past because of election results, police shootings and Super Bowl outcomes.

Today, apart from the traffic all was quiet and peaceful. As I left downtown Oakland to enter Berkeley there was a distinct change to both the road quality and the buildings quality and upkeep, this was getting closer to the Berkeley University quarter. This academic powerhouse of 40,000 students has resulted in a mixture of swanky student apartments and exclusive properties for the support and teaching staff.

La Loma Park was rising on the side of the 1,200ft peak, which was covered by woodlands and sleepy quiet houses perched on the flanks of the steep sides. I started climbing up this alpine scene which became very steep; very soon, my granny gear was not low enough in some places so I had to push the bike along the gutter of the road. Beside me looking down the growing hill the log cabin homes along the side were being held in place by a network of poles stuck into the ground, not sure if I would be happy living in one of those buildings given the recent earthquake in the area.

At one point when pushing the bike the rear wheel got stuck between the road and the sidewalk, it was stuck fast and would not budge. I tugged it forwards and backwards and it would still not move, eventually I had to let some air out of the tyre and remove all the luggage to clear it from its vice like grip. I re-filled the air and checked the wheel was still running true and noted a few nicks on the rim, hopefully this would have no negative effect, how wrong I was.

The Alpine climb continued past exclusive houses with magnificent views across to San Francisco behind me. I managed to cycle the rest of the hill up as its gradient reduced a little and I did get some strange looks from the residents that I saw, I think they were not used to seeing a cyclist on their steep quiet hill, especially not an English one. The woods closed in around me which was a welcome break from the searing sun as I was finding this climb hard and demanding.

Then the road name changed to Wildcat Canyon Road which now crossed through the Tilden Regional Park with its mandatory 30mph limit, although as usual it was often ignored and sometimes doubled. The bright yellow diagonal signs every quarter mile told everyone to "share the road" with a picture of a bicycle emblazoned on it but in my experience, it would have been better to change that to "loathed to share the road" with a red cross through the bicycle-it would have been more accurate. It was a nasty twisty road with steep ups and downs along the plateau but with great woodland views if one could find the time to look, I was more concerned with the happenings on this road. Cars sliced past at high speed with fast oncoming vehicles approaching, forcing everyone to quickly adjust road positions before a blasting of horns was given out as a protest. I took refuge to calm down at the aptly named Inspiration Point car park.

This vantage point opened to a massive vista of peaks and passes over the next ten miles with lakes, fields and towns all displayed. A motorcyclist called Steve was also enjoying the view and after noting the Union Jack on my bike came over and had a chat. He had worked in the UK for a few years and was keen to catch up on some gossip, which turned into a debate over the recent Brexit referendum result; he was personally disappointed with the outcome and thought that the British people were duped by politicians who should have known better.

We then spoke about motorcycling in the USA and how dangerous it is becoming, which is why he sold his heavy Harley Davidson to get his current lighter and more manoeuvrable trials motorbike. He feels that this helps him to avoid potential accidents caused by unobservant drivers. He wished me bon-voyage and disappeared down the hill on his motorbike still smoking his cigarette as he went.

Then a car turned up and the women driver got out and went to the back of the car and lifted off her mountain bike off the rear rack. She said that she often drove up to this point and cycled in a circle completely around the peak using the various bike trails available as it was good exercise and more importantly far safer than being on the road. Was this the future of cycling? I thought, everyone driving to a safe location, trail or track then enjoying their cycle ride and driving back safe in the confines of a metal box. This thought, together with various news reports I had previously read back in the UK started to form a pattern. Such as instances where a cyclist was knocked off their bike and one of the witnesses said that they should not have been on the road as it was far too busy. Or drivers reporting that they had to get really close to cyclists as there was not enough room available, instead of waiting for a space. This worrying trend of cycling being recommended as a hobby or pastime that should be carried out in the safe confines of an off-road facility is growing. Before long it will be seen only as a stunt-person's pursuit if you choose to cycle on the road, especially to just get from A to B for the fun of it.

I started off down the hill and a sharp bend was approaching so I braked hard to slow down and heard a "clunk-clunk-clunk" which was also reverberating through the bike.

I released the brakes and it stopped, front brake only and no noise heard, back brake only and again "clunk-clunk-clunk" came back. It sounded and felt very bad, I was rummaging through my brain trying to think what it could be, spokes? Wheel bearing? Worn out brake-blocks? Yes, that's it. I pulled over and inspected the rear brake-blocks but they were virtually brand new and had many thousands of miles left in them.

I checked every spoke for tension and they were all fine, then I felt the wheel for any side play and again everything was perfect. I got back on the bike and continued the long downhill with the "clunk-clunk-clunk" soundtrack playing all the way down. As it only happened when rear braking I tended to try and brake more front only where possible so I could get down this hill and have another inspection and perhaps discover a cause.

I did check it a few more times and each time I could not find the cause, it had come from nowhere to be loud and it could be felt through the bike, it was most unusual. There was only about 10 miles remaining on the journey to Neil's house so I started to get very philosophical and thought it's better to happen now within the final 10 miles as opposed to the tours first 10 miles.

The road now had a marked cycle path on its side so things got less tense and more enjoyable around me. The high hills all around had the road cut into their sides and this highway weaved around the edges of the peaks, then this changed, as the road went straight over the top of the next hill, I had to ascend once again. It was a hard slog but fortunately the road was very quiet so there was no rush and about half way up I saw another licence plate just waiting to be recovered.

This was a California plate, very discoloured and battered but I was sure that I could clean and straighten it when I got it home. Down the hill the other side the "clunk-clunk-clunk" returned during braking and then I realised how foolish I had been. The small nicks in the rear rim made whilst the wheel was wedged in the sidewalk above Berkeley were the culprits. When braking the rear brake-blocks have the smooth rim surface interrupted by the small nicks, a bit like a scratched record to a stylus and this was making the annoying noise.

I knew that there was nothing that could be done and it would resolve itself after a few hundred miles when the rim around the nicks would be worn down to its equal height, gosh I felt better, my wheel was not going to fall off after all.

My route kept passing over and under US route 24 with its six lanes of traffic maintaining the awful ambient noise. Then just after Lafayette I picked up an off-road cycle track which was an old converted railway line for walkers and cyclist. It was quiet and blissful with the only threat from the occasional errant dog running across my path. Disused cycle paths are great for cycling but this one was very well hidden with no signs directing potential cyclists to use it, once again it was thanks to the GPS, that has now just about made up for its previous disappointments. Back on quiet roads and crossing over the Interstate 680 and before I knew it I had turned up at Neil's front porch.

My ride in the USA was now complete, to a total of 1,180 miles and without any major problems with bike or body and as such I was feeling very content with life, the universe and everything. I met Neil's family for the first time in about 15 years and we caught up with all that both he and I had missed from each other's lives in that time-it obviously took a while but lubricated by beer it was great.

Ride Data	
Date	16/5/18
Cycling Distance (Miles)	38
Cycling Time (Hours)	4:29
Average speed (mph)	8.4
Elevation Gain (feet)	3,200

Data-Totals	
Cycling Distance (Miles) Kilometres	1,185 (1910)
Cycling Time (Hours in saddle)	144 (6 days)
Days cycling	25
Elevation Gain (feet)	52,225 (9 miles)
Number of Punctures	1

Chapter 30

Life in San Francisco bay area

Neil is a self-employed inspector on construction sites in the bay area for both health and safety and environmental issues. Fortunately, I used to teach health and safety courses in college to students and I was also a qualified health and safety inspector for the teaching union, so I donned a hard hat, put on a Hi-Viz jacket and grabbed a clipboard and went to work with Neil on his site inspections for a few days, a sort of busman's holiday I suppose.

It was incredibly interesting to see the differences between residential construction sites in the UK and the USA, the main one is that houses are all built in wood in the bay area, which is the material I would want my house to be built of whilst in an earthquake zone.

The size of the houses are so much bigger as well however, given that wood is cheaper and lighter than brick that may be a factor. We visited many sites all over a wide area which required a lot of driving to get to and I think once we were there the staff and foreman of each site were suitably impressed to have two qualified British staff inspect their sites.

Driving on the freeway and interstate with Neil around the San Francisco area was scary, not because of Neil's driving as he is a good driver and he even used to race cars years ago, no it was everyone else. I wrote this after one particularly terrifying day on the road to help calm my nerves:

The roads in America from being inside a car:

-It felt like being in a wilder but real version of the wacky races, it starts on the on-ramp when you accelerate into the massive throng of 6-8 lanes of all types of vehicles. Everyone seems hell bent on closing all gaps that exist on the road surface, in fact the road is often fully obscured by cars and lorries moving snake like to their various destinations. Licence plates indicate their home-states such as Idaho, Florida or the more common California plate.

Maximum lane room is provided and where not available there are double decker roads or bridges that cocoon the vehicles into a long stream of metal on the move over or through hills, over cities, over and under water, nothing stands in the way of the ever-pressing American dream of making money.

Take that call, drink that coffee, doesn't matter- your vehicle is your domain, feeling like breaking the speed limit by 30 mph? Go for it! The reflection of society and its risk takers and chancers can be found on the freeway ever striving forward.

We went to Neil's local bar to unwind which was in Alamo and to me it was like a normal British pub, no food, only drinks, unless you count the chips on the counter.

Only one guest draft beer is available at a time unless you want bottled beer. The regulars made me feel very welcome and we watched the golf on the TV above the bar, was I in *Moe's* bar? No this was *Cheers* as everyone knew your name.

The owner/landlord told me that the local paper called him the other day and advised him that they had been awarded the number one dive bar in the east bay area. I said congratulations to him but it was the exact opposite he wanted, as to be awarded this status is not good for business or acceptance within the local businesses, such a shame.

Chapter 31

Going home

Part of my earlier planning for the trip even included arranging to collect a bike cardboard box to bring the bike home in.

The local bike shop was only a few miles away from Neil's house, so I went in and spoke to Tony at the California Bike & Snowboard shop and told him about the trip I had done across the three states. He was so impressed that he gave the box and many of the spacer parts for free, many thanks Tony. Back at Neil's I started to dismantle the bike but found out that the box was slightly smaller than the one I used on the way out so I had to take the front forks off as well.

This required the vintage quill stem to be removed but I found out it was totally seized to the tube lining; however, I was still able to remove the forks successfully.

On the day of the flight Neil drove me to San Francisco International airport and we bid farewell hoping and promising that we will see each other a lot sooner next time.

I grabbed an $8 trolley! and put the bike box at the back and the large bag containing the panniers on the front, only to find that it would not fit through the security posts out the front of the terminal building as it was hideously wide. After moving through the security barrier by carrying the box over it, I was in the airport departures area, I found a seat and waited a few hours before Virgin Atlantic check-in opened.

When it opened check in it went smoothly and I watched the bike and bag disappear into the airport system.

The overnight flight back was in a Boeing 787 Dreamliner that was super quiet and comfortable and the copious food was exceptional. Back in Heathrow airport I built the bike and handed the box to the helpful cleaner who would dispose of it on my behalf.

The quick Heathrow Express train whisked me to Paddington train station and then I boarded the Great Western Railway train to Plymouth.

I sat being amazed at how green our countryside is and enjoyed listening to the various British accents around me on the train, I was back by 7pm, and I had concluded my USA quest, now where next?

Chapter 32

Observations from the USA:

I note some of the items that I thought strange/unusual or
noteworthy.

- Light switches are all upside down and are toggle
  types.

- Taps are sometimes difficult to use as they are all
  shared mixer tap configurations that you either
  push, pull, yank, twist or generally shout at to get
  water.

- No hotels have water plugs in either the bath or
  sink-take one with you.

- All cars sound horn once or twice when being
  locked/unlocked, this is very annoying and I am
  not sure how people put up with this at 3am, I
  know I didn't.

- Traffic lights take an age to change for both cars
  and pedestrian crossings.

- Traffic lights go straight from red to green, no
  amber; it's like the start of the Monaco grand
  prix.

- USA flags are everywhere, the bigger the better.

- The roads are full of both potholes, cracks and open groves.

- TV is full of adverts and may contain some programmes.

- TV adverts for medical drugs must state all possible side effects-it often sounds like a horror film when they are given.

- Power sockets and hairdryers are to be found in the bathroom.

- All money bills are the same colour and size, so take some reading glasses!

- The few roundabouts that are around confuse people, so most have stop signs in place of yield signs (give-way).

- The price you see in the shop is not what you pay. Tax is added afterwards and changes depending where you are.

- Gas (petrol) must be paid for first before you can put it in your car.

- It is not called cycling in the USA it's called bicycling.

- Ground floor does not exist; it is called the first floor.

- You can turn right at a red light (unless signs prohibit it).

- Crossing the road on foot away from a crossing is called Jaywalking and is illegal.

- Under 18 year olds must wear a cycle helmet.

- Most shopping centres and restaurants have signs stating that "no guns are allowed".

- When driving, you can pass vehicles on both the inside and outside on the freeway/interstates.

- Cyclists must use the shoulder on the allowable interstates.

- Places that sell drinks and no food are called "Dive bars" and are frowned upon.

- Chips are called fries, crisps are called chips, football is called soccer, and toilets are called bathrooms.

- Washing machines are never found in the kitchen as that is regarded as unclean and dirty in the US.

- Kilometres are not recognised; in fact, this applies to the entire metric system.

- American toilet bowls are huge and full of water (13.5 litres, UK toilets use 6 litres), and they sound like a plane toilet when being flushed.

- Cannabis use is legal in some states and the number is growing, as is the number of farms that produce it.

- Some states such as Arizona and Florida have no specific laws banning mobile phone use whilst driving.

- Indicators or turn signals as they are called can be yellow or just a flashing brake light-there is no consistency.

Chapter 33

Tempted to cycle tour? some sage advice…

Any bike is suitable for cycle touring as long as you feel comfortable and confident riding it, the type is not important, it just needs to have strong wheels, good tyres, reliable brakes, working lights and gears suitable for your intended destination.

On a tour the luggage weight should be kept physically as low as possible and on the bike (near the axle) and balanced both left and right. It is also important that you do a "shake down" and take the bike out with the luggage and the maximum weight you expect to carry (I used lots of 2 litre coke bottles filled with water distributed around the panniers to replicate the weight).

If on your tour you plan on doing say 40 miles a day, then do at least 20 miles a day for a week fully laden as that will show up any problems with either the luggage, rack, bike or your body.

One of the most important things to remember is that your body will hurt so make sure that you can recognise niggle pain versus serious damage pain and be prepared to rest if you need to. To be honest, your level of fitness at the start of a long tour is never enough unless you happen to live on your bike. Therefore, build your route to incorporate this, start with lower mileages and increase them as the tour develops. If it's hilly and mainly uphill then do less that day, if its downhill for 30 miles and you expect a tailwind again take that into account and perhaps do more miles that day. By doing this you are building up stamina and fitness, I guarantee you will feel fitter at the end of the ride than the start, every time.

Try to keep all your valuables in a bar bag which is right in front of you all day and easy to unclip and carry around in supermarkets etc. What you regard as valuables is up to you but consider if everything was stolen what do you need to; 1. continue the tour or 2.get home. My valuables were below 3kg in weight and consisted of; passport, money, wallet with credit card, cameras, GoPro, phone, iPad, paper maps, painkillers and charging adaptor and cables.

Once you have decided on all your clothes etc. that you will take then spread it all out over a floor and here's the difficult bit-try to take out and discard 50% of it, you will thank me- I promise.

The issue of tools is always tricky as you could take so many tools and spares so that you are needlessly weighed down, again this is personal preference based on your bikes reliability and history coupled with your own knowledge to deal with a problem.

Where you are touring also dictates your tools and spares so that if you are going to be totally remote with no passing traffic you need to take more, I was on roads that were often empty but at least there was some traffic that I knew would pass me...eventually, that I could flag down and plead help/transport from. So, I took a multi-tool that has all the Allen keys you will need and has a spoke key and chain tool built in, the spare spokes which I labelled and put in a plastic bag and wedged inside the saddle stem (you will need 6 in total, 2 for the front wheel and 4 for the rear being 2 for each side as they are different lengths). A puncture repair kit, a spare inner tube, a couple of pairs of disposable gloves, chain oil, two small working pumps that you know how to use, couple of chain links, spare inner cables for brakes and gears, small cable cutters and cable clamp ends. If you take spares then you also need to know how to fit them, so practice at home, do research, quiz the bike shop, as the old adage of knowledge is power is crucial for running repairs on the road.

Please do not panic as I have toured on many bikes that have only been maintained by me and they have never seen a bike shop in their entire life and I only know the basics and what I have picked up over the years. Crucially, you are unlikely to get a major breakdown if you look after and listen to your bike and fix any small issues before they become major breaks. Most major faults will give some small indication such as a squeak, clunk, click or crunch before they finally expire.

The bicycle is an amazing invention that can withstand many thousands of miles with very little maintenance required, the main things that do wear out are; wheels with rim brakes, -check the wear indicator, brake-blocks or pads if disc brakes, inner cables for gears and brakes, replace before they break where possible and all the transmission gear covering cassette, chain-rings and chain.

It's best to replace these all at the same time so that they wear in naturally together as opposed to the "clunk-clunk" wearing in method.

Tyres should have enough good tread for the expected mileage and terrain, replace if unsure, use wider tyres if poor road/trail surfaces are expected and narrower if a good surface is expected, go for the middle if unsure.

You WILL experience punctures, sometimes far too many, if that happens check the tread/quality of your tyres-swap tyres from back to front to extend wear if required. I always use *Schwalbe Marathon Plus* tyres as although they wear quicker they are bullet proof against punctures. Make sure that you are also adept at fixing punctures, practice if not and only use your spare inner tube if you cannot repair it with a patch, if you do this get a replacement spare inner tube as soon as possible.

Items that rarely need changing but if the bike is abused or has high mileage then these may require attention; crank bearings (lots of types in use -so do your research) pedals and headset bearings.

We are now in an age of information at our fingertips via the Internet and that has made access to good quality information easier than ever before.

We can learn by watching videos, looking at pictures and reading accounts of others and viewing specialised sites, I suggest that you now have everything that you need to plan, train, and enjoy your own quest; however long or short it may be-good luck and "enjoy the freedom!"

Paul Bunce
www.saltash.com